TRICKY PUZZLES for SMART KIDS

Dr Shireen Stephen holds a PhD in Health Psychology and an MPhil and MSc in Applied Psychology. She is a counselling psychologist, researcher, writer and editor. She is well-known for her episodic memory of remembering dates and connected events. She is also renowned for her auditory memory of remembering clients and their counselling sessions—even years later—without taking down any notes!

She is the author of *Smart Guide for Awesome Memory, The 4-Week Memory Challenge, Train Your Brain: Ultimate Memory Hacks* and *The Ultimate Brain-Boosting Toolkit*.

TRICKY PUZZLES for SMART KIDS

SHIREEN STEPHEN

RUPA

Published by
Rupa Publications India Pvt. Ltd 2022
7/16, Ansari Road, Daryaganj
New Delhi 110002

Sales Centres:
Allahabad Bengaluru Chennai
Hyderabad Jaipur Kathmandu
Kolkata Mumbai

Copyright © Shireen Stephen 2022

The views and opinions expressed in this book are the author's own and the facts are as reported by her which have been verified to the extent possible, and the publishers are not in any way liable for the same.

All rights reserved.
No part of this publication may be reproduced, transmitted, or stored in a retrieval system, in any form or by any means, electronic, mechanical, photocopying, recording or otherwise, without the prior permission of the publisher.

ISBN: 978-93-5520-473-8

Second impression 2023

10 9 8 7 6 5 4 3 2

Printed in India

This book is sold subject to the condition that it shall not, by way of trade or otherwise, be lent, resold, hired out, or otherwise circulated, without the publisher's prior consent, in any form of binding or cover other than that in which it is published.

To my daughters Shifrah and Annika, the original queens at making up puzzles and riddles. With all my love, hugs and kisses.

INTRODUCTION

Do you know what the world's oldest puzzle is? Well, in recorded history, it is said to be a labyrinth (pronounced as la-buh-rih-nth) puzzle, which dates back to more than 4,300 years! A labyrinth is a flat circle or square which has a path that winds its way to the centre and out again. Each path is unique for each labyrinth, and it is easy to get lost as the pathways can twist and turn and lead to dead ends. However, if you follow certain rules, you can make it to the centre and back without getting lost. Thankfully, in modern times, we don't have to physically walk through labyrinths in order to have fun—we can solve puzzles right in the comfort of our own houses!

Much like the labyrinths of ancient Greece and Rome, this book contains puzzles that have specific rules. Following these rules, you'll be able to get to the heart of the puzzle and solve it easily. All it takes is a little thought and effort from you! This book also contains bonus riddles, brain-teasers or fun facts at the end of most puzzles to keep your brain buzzing and active for the rest of the day.

Puzzles and brain-teasers have many benefits. They help keep your brain fit and strong, improve your memory, focus and concentration, and can also spark your creativity! What's more, they can help with your schoolwork too! Understanding the logic behind these puzzles and applying similar logic and rules in school, you can solve any mathematics problem that your teacher gives you!

How to Use This Book

This book contains 100 puzzles and games. Many more bonus secret codes, brain-teasers, riddles or fun activities are included after most of the main puzzles. You can solve the puzzles in any order, but since the puzzles start easy and increase in difficulty as you go along, it is recommended that you start at the very beginning and work your way through the book.

Solving puzzles, brain-teasers and riddles for at least half an hour a day is all it takes to keep your mind healthy and fit. Each puzzle will take about 10 minutes or more to solve; so try and do at least three puzzles a day. You can time yourself, if you wish. There is a space provided at the end of each puzzle to record the time that you have taken to solve it.

While it's good to solve as many puzzles as you can, solving too many at once may make your brain tired, which may lead to mistakes. Try and take a short break for a few minutes between puzzles to drink water or eat a snack. This will help keep your brain fresh and ready to solve more puzzles!

Some exercises may seem simple and some difficult; but don't let this stop you from trying them all out! Read the rules and instructions at the beginning of each puzzle before you start. If you get stuck and cannot figure out how to solve a puzzle, read the rules again and look at the example of the solved puzzled, if provided. If you are still puzzled, take a quick peek at the answer section at the end of the book and try to solve the rest of the puzzle by yourself. All answers are provided at the end of the book. In case you still find it difficult, ask an adult or an older sibling to help you. Try not to flip to the answers. You should try your best to solve the puzzles first. Remember, you have all the answers within you already—you just need to think for a bit!

Most exercises require you to write or draw something; so keep a pencil and eraser ready. You can either solve the puzzles directly on the book or use a sheet of paper to work out some of the puzzles. All exercises have a time limit, so having a watch or stopwatch handy may help.

While this book contains many exercises that will keep you busy for weeks, solving puzzles needs to be an activity that can be carried out throughout your life. Try and solve puzzles in daily newspapers, magazines and websites. If a certain type of puzzle interests you, try and find it online. Make sure you keep challenging yourself by working out increasingly difficult puzzles.

This book is designed for children aged 8 and above. The whole premise of solving puzzles is to have fun while challenging your brain. So, sit back, relax and enjoy yourself!

TANGRAM SHAPES

Cut out the seven shapes below. These shapes will come in handy while solving some of the puzzles in this book. If you happen to have Tangram puzzle blocks with you, you can use those as well.

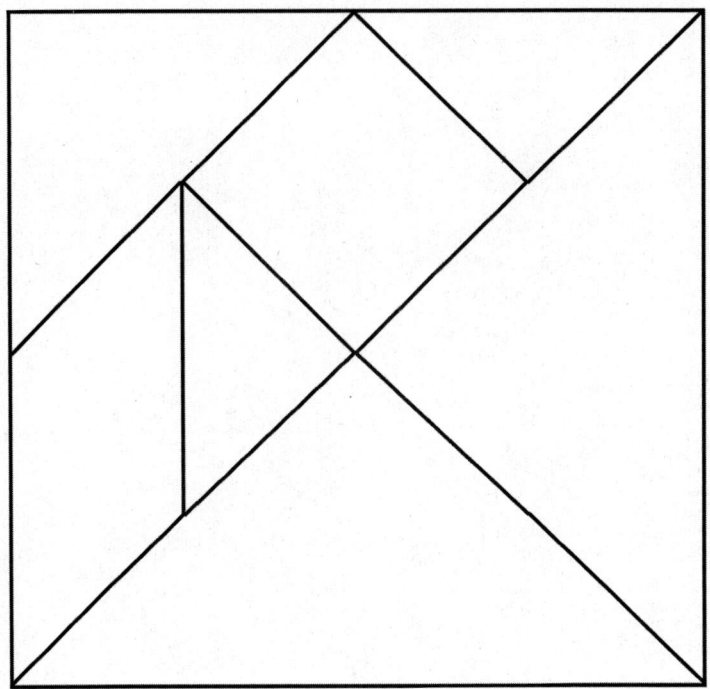

SUPER EASY PUZZLES

PUZZLE 1: MAZE AMAZE

TIME LIMIT: 10 MINUTES

Find your way out of this tricky maze. Start at the entrance and work your way to the exit.

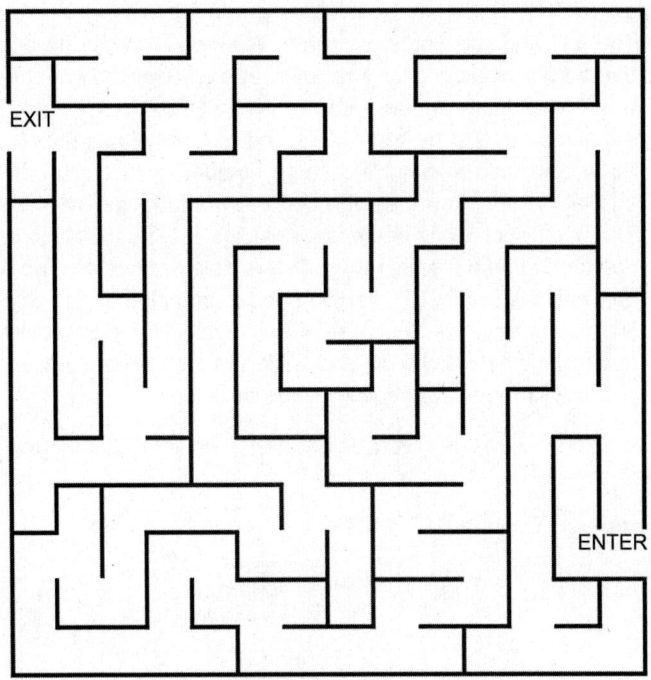

Time taken: _____

Fun Fact

In ancient times, there was no difference between a labyrinth and a maze. However, there is a distinction in modern times. A labyrinth has only one path that twists and turns and leads to the centre. This path does not have branches. You can walk to its very centre and then use the same path to find your way out again. So, the entrance is also the exit.

    A maze, on the other hand, is a confusing pathway that has many branches, choices of pathways and dead ends. While you can use a pathway to get to the centre, you can exit at a different location.

PUZZLE 2: WORD LADDERS

A word ladder is a sequence of words formed by just changing one letter at a time.

Rules
1. The first and last words are given. Working your way up or down the ladder, change only **one** letter in each word to get the next word—eventually ending with the final word.
2. All words have to be real words and not made-up words.
3. All words need to have the same number of letters as the first and last words. You cannot make the words longer or shorter.
4. The number of rungs in the ladder indicates how many words are needed to make the final word. In example 1, there are two rungs between BAT and CUP; so you need to complete the puzzle with two connecting words or less. Similarly, in example 2, there are three rungs between DOG and CAT; so you need to complete the puzzle with three connecting words or less.

Look at the examples given below to get an idea of how to solve this puzzle.

Example 1: Change BAT to CUP

B	A	T
C	A	T
C	U	T
C	U	P

Example 2: Change DOG to CAT

D	O	G
C	O	G
C	O	P
C	A	P
C	A	T

TIME LIMIT: 10 MINUTES

A) Turn this RUG into a HAT within two steps. Some clues are given to help you.

R	U	G
H	A	T

A warm embrace.

A witch in fairy tales.

B) Pour the TEA into the CUP within four steps.

T	E	A
C	U	P

Two ___ ___ ___ s in a pod.

To stroke or pat affectionately.

I ___ ___ ___ my hand under water.

Baby dog.

Time taken: _____

Fun Fact

Word ladder is a word game invented by Lewis Carroll, the author of *Alice's Adventures in Wonderland*. He invented this game on Christmas day in 1877. These puzzles are featured in *The New York Times* crossword puzzles even today, more than 140 years later!

Can you invent your own word ladder? Let's see how many rungs you can make!

PUZZLE 3: DOMINO TWIST

Have you ever played Dominoes before? If you have, you already know how to play this game. If you haven't, don't worry as the rules are very simple and explained below.

Rules
1. Place the five dominoes in the spaces provided.
2. Each domino piece can be rotated to fit into the space.
3. The domino piece that you place must match the piece already provided. For example, if the edge piece has five dots on it, the domino that you place next to it also needs to have five dots.

Hints
1. If you have domino pieces at home, you can use those to help you solve this puzzle.
2. You can trace out the five domino pieces on a different piece of paper, cut them out and then place them on the puzzle. This makes it easier to rotate the pieces to see where they may fit.

Look at the example below to see how to match the dominoes.

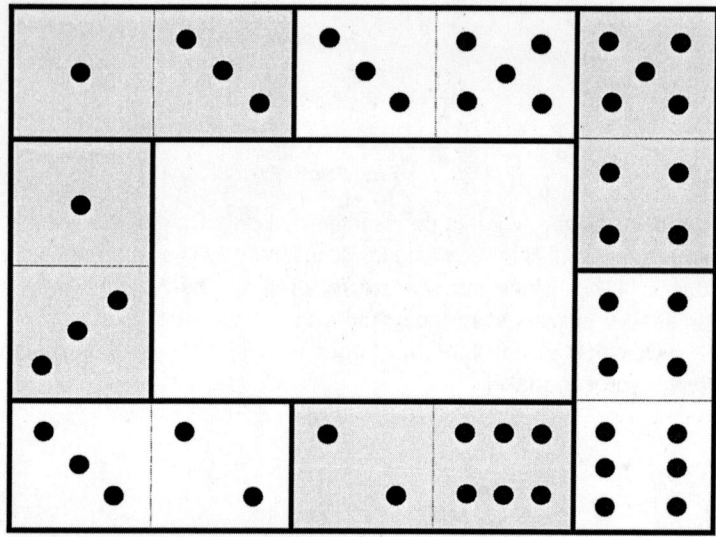

TIME LIMIT: 10 MINUTES

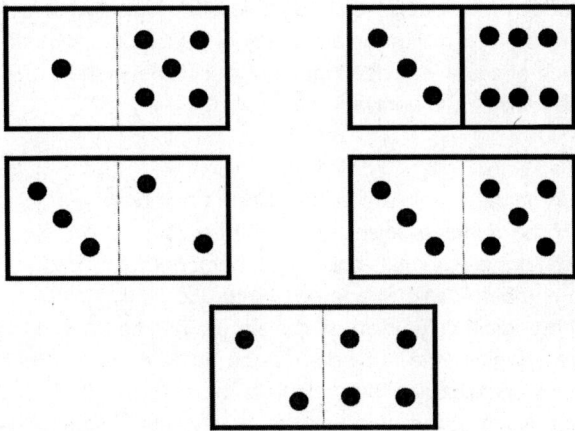

Place the dominoes above in the figure below.

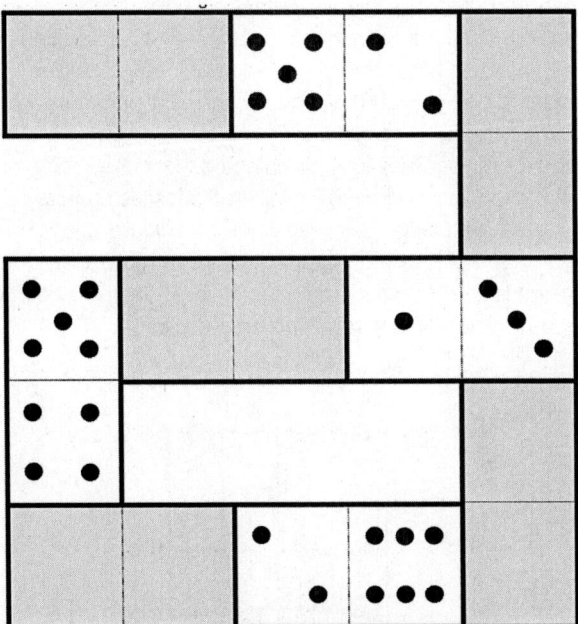

Time taken: _____

PUZZLE 4: MINI-SUDOKU

Mini Sudoku is a puzzle that requires pure logic to solve. There is only one solution. Given below is a mini Sudoku puzzle that involves a 4x4 grid of squares divided into 2x2 blocks. Fill in the blank squares with the correct numbers.

Rules
1. Every square should contain just one number.
2. Only the numbers from 1 to 4 can be used.
3. Each 2x2 block must contain all numbers from 1 to 4. None of the numbers can be repeated in the block.
4. Each vertical column must contain the numbers from 1 to 4 only once. None of the numbers can be repeated in the column.
5. Each horizontal row must contain the numbers from 1 to 4 only once. None of the numbers can be repeated in the rows.

Hints
1. When you start the Sudoku puzzle, some squares will already be filled with numbers. Use those numbers as clues for blank squares.
2. Start by identifying the blank squares that give you a definite answer. Once you do this, you will be able to deduce other blank squares around that number.
3. Some blank squares may initially look like they may hold more than one possible number. Pencil in all possible numbers and move on to the next blank square. Once you figure out a number for certain, go back to the squares that have more than one answer and erase that number from that square. This will help eliminate numbers until you arrive at just one answer.

Look at the example. The shaded squares were blank squares that were filled.

4	1	2	3
3	2	4	1
2	3	1	4
1	4	3	2

TIME LIMIT: 10 MINUTES

A)

		1	
3		4	
	3		4
	4		

B)

			2
	3	4	
	4	2	
3			

Time taken: _____

Fun Activity: Thinking outside the box

Nine dots are placed in three rows with three dots in each row as shown in the picture. These nine dots must be connected by four straight connected lines, without lifting up your pen or pencil.

PUZZLE 5: COIN BOARD

Place two coins on each row so that each row, column and the two main diagonals contain only two coins.

Rules
1. You can place only one coin per square.
2. Each row, column and the two main diagonals must contain only two coins.

Hints
1. You can use real coins for this puzzle or simply shade in the squares on which you would place a coin. You need 10 coins.
2. Start at the centre and work your way outwards.

Look at the example given below to get an idea of the completed puzzle.

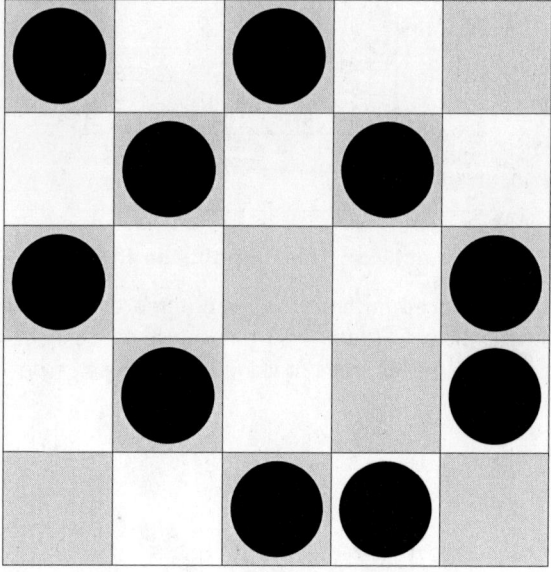

TIME LIMIT: 10 MINUTES

Solve the puzzles below. Four coins are already placed to help you get started.

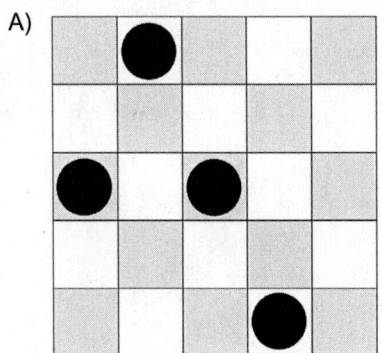

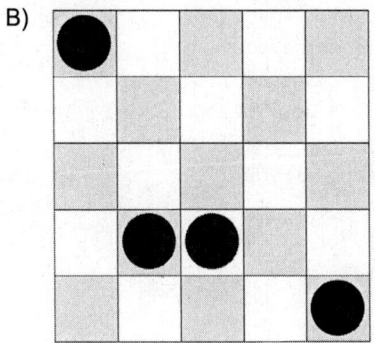

Time taken: _____

Bonus Game: Coin Touch

Now that you have your coins out, try this game. Can you arrange four coins in such a way that every coin is touching all other coins?

PUZZLE 6: WORD SWIRL

TIME LIMIT: 10 MINUTES

How many words of four or more letters can you make from the following word swirl?

Rules
1. Follow the clues below to find the word.
2. Each word must have the centre letter (C) in it.
3. All words have to be real words and not made up.

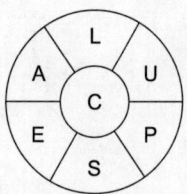

Clues
1. Santa __ __ __ __ __. (5 letters)
2. 'I can't be at two __ __ __ __ __ __ (locations) at once.' (6 letters)
3. 'Not all superheroes wear __ __ __ __ __ (cloaks).' (5 letters)
4. __ __ __ __ __ and effect. (5 letters)
5. The physical universe beyond Earth's atmosphere (outer __ __ __ __ __). (5 letters)
6. When you applaud, you __ __ __ __ your hands. (4 letters)
7. 'Tie your shoe __ __ __ __ __ or you'll trip over them.' (5 letters)
8. Another word for a measuring ruler. __ __ __ __ __ (5 letters)
9. Hints that detectives use to solve crimes. __ __ __ __ __ (5 letters)
10. Can you guess the 7-letter word? __ __ __ __ __ __ __
    (**Hint:** It's a pill or tablet that comes in a soluble case.)

Time taken: _____

PUZZLE 7: FOLDING CUBES   TIME LIMIT: 10 MINUTES

The following figures are called cube nets. How many of them can form three-dimensional cubes when they are folded?

Rules
1. Imagine that each shape is folded along its lines. You will have to manipulate the shapes in your mind and see which cube nets form cubes. If you find it hard to do this, trace or draw the shapes on a separate piece of paper and physically fold them on their lines to see if it makes a cube.
2. There should not be any overlapping flaps.

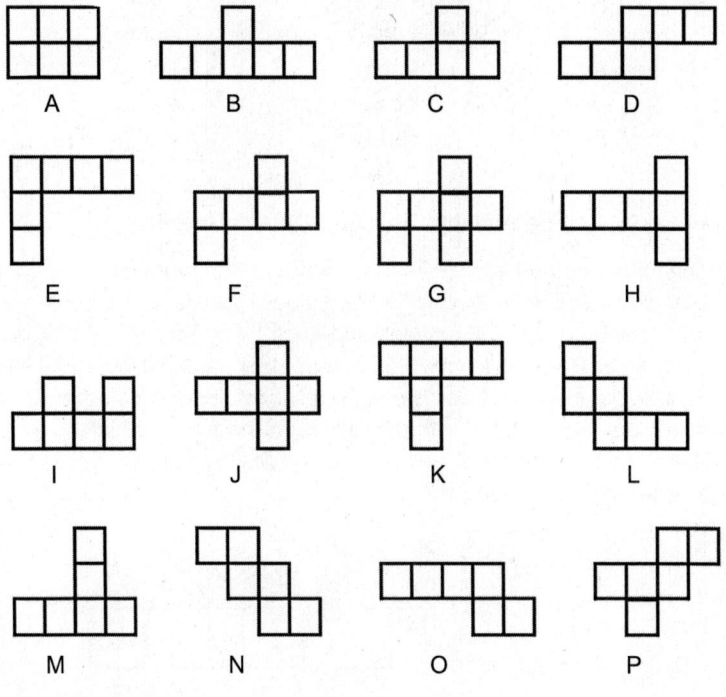

Time taken: _____

PUZZLE 8: WORD SEARCH– P

Find and circle the following words in the word search puzzle on the next page. All words begin with the letter P. The words can be found horizontally, vertically or diagonally—in any direction (back to front or bottom to top). There are 30 words to find in 30 minutes so try and find all the words as quickly as possible!

- Provide
- Private
- Problem
- Present
- Perform
- Popular
- Perfect
- Prevent
- Patient
- Picture
- Pattern
- Portion
- Print
- Prevail
- Paradox
- Piping
- Pottery
- Poetry
- Plant
- Pivot
- Prompt
- Phrase
- Polite
- Puzzled
- Pillow
- Potter
- Pencil
- Pepper
- Patron
- Pant

Fun Activity: Thinking Outside the Box

The three houses below need to be supplied with three utility services: Water, Internet and Electricity. Each house needs to be connected to all three utilities. This means that each house and utility will have three lines. The challenge is to connect them without crossing lines through houses or utilities. The houses cannot share lines either. Draw nine lines connecting the three houses to the three utilities.

Hint: Look at this puzzle as a three-dimensional puzzle rather than a two-dimensional one.

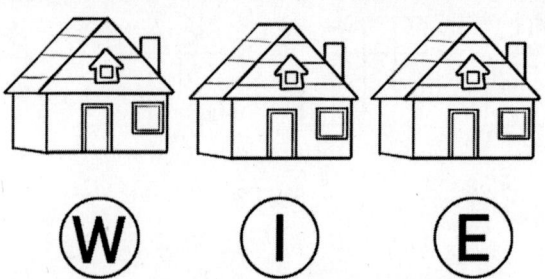

TIME LIMIT: 30 MINUTES

P	P	A	R	A	D	O	X	N	X	T	H	I			
G	I	Q	Z	M	X	P	B	O	N	N	B	P	G	P	
H	P	U	Z	P	E	N	C	I	L	D	V	A	F	L	P
F	I	I	X	U	O	H	R	T	H	B	R	T	J	H	F	S
I	N	D	W	Z	U	P	E	R	F	E	C	T	I	P	E	D	R
D	G	B	B	Z	X	B	H	O	Q	J	T	E	E	H	D	K	W
B	Q	P	I	L	L	O	W	P	Z	Z	D	R	P	R	O	M	P	T
A	J	E	M	E	Z	D						N	E	A	F	J	G	G
P	L	F	B	D	O	P							P	S	P	P	S	G	J
K	I	D	V	T	O	K							P	E	H	A	R	S	G
L	A	G	C	T	G	T							E	R	U	T	C	I	P
A	V	E	T	R	B	U							R	F	T	I	T	A	D
D	E	E	M	U	P	T						V	U	C	E	E	Y	P
E	R	T	T	I	P	J	J	E	G	O	Y	Q	T	N	R	N	Q
T	P	E	R	F	O	R	M	U	K	P	R	E	V	E	N	T	U
P	J	Q	V	E	P	T	G	D	J	T	L	M	R	H	U	U
A	D	W	Q	F	U	P	P	F	N	E	R	A	E	F	Q	T
T	Z	E	T	I	L	O	P	H	M	F	A	B	N	K	H
R	Z	L	I	H	A	E	G	P	R	E	S	E	N	T
O	Q	K	V	R	R	T
N	B	H	G	Y	P	R
P	O	T	T	E	R	Y
R	T	T	F	G	F	M
U	E	R	D	U	I	E
P	A	N	T	Q	T	L
E	L	Y	O	A	E	B
G	G	R	V	J	J	O
J	E	I	I	M	F	R
K	R	P	P	N	J	P
P	R	O	V	I	D	E

Time taken: _____

PUZZLE 9: SLITHERLINKS

Slitherlink puzzles are also known as fences, takegaki, loop the loop and suriza. This is a puzzle that uses a square or rectangular grid that contains the numbers 1, 2 and 3 scattered around it. The objective of this puzzle is to use the numbers as guides to help you draw horizontal or vertical 'fences' around the entire puzzle to form a simple loop, with no open ends. The numbers 1, 2 and 3 inside the squares represent the number of fences or loops around that particular number. This puzzle requires pure logic to solve and does not involve any guess work.

Rules
1. The fence or loop has to be a single continuous line throughout the puzzle. All line segments must be connected.
2. The loop cannot touch or cross itself at any point. It also cannot be left open at any point.
3. The number of fences around a particular number should correspond to that number. For example, if the number is 2, then only two fences can be drawn around that number, either to the left, right, top or bottom of the number.
4. If there is no number in a square, you can draw any number of lines surrounding that square in order to connect the loop to numbered squares.

Hints
1. If the number of fences surrounding a square correspond to the number in the square, all other possible horizontal and vertical lines surrounding that square can be eliminated.
2. Start with a number which points to a definite fence. For example, if there is a 3 in the corner, you know for sure that the two outside edges need to be drawn. That leaves only the two inside edges, which can be deduced using the other numbers surrounding it.

Example:

2	1	2	2		
2				3	1
2	2		3	2	
3	3	1		2	2
1	2				2
3		3	2	2	3

TIME LIMIT: 10 MINUTES

A)

			3
	2		
		3	1
2	1	3	

B)

	1	3		
2		2	2	2
2				2
3				
	3			3

C)

1			3		3
	3	2	0		2
2			2		
			2	1	
3	1			3	
	3				

Time taken: _____

PUZZLE 10: HAPPINESS REVERSE CROSSWORD

TIME LIMIT: 10 MINUTES

In a reverse crossword, all the answers are already given; you will just need to place each answer in its correct slot. This puzzle requires pure logic to solve and does not involve any guess work. Fit all the synonyms (words with the same meaning) of the word 'Happy' into their correct boxes.

Hint
Start with the word that you know will definitely fit into its correct slot and work your way around the crossword puzzle from there.

10-letter words
Enraptured

9-letter words
Contented
Exuberant

8-letter words
Cheerful

6-letter words
Elated
Blithe

5-letter words
Merry
Smile

4-letter words
Rapt

2-letter words
Up

Time taken: _____

PUZZLE 11: WORD PYRAMID

TIME LIMIT: 10 MINUTES

Beginning at the top, add a letter to a box at each step, moving towards the bottom seven-letter word. Solve each clue and write the answer in each corresponding row.

Rules
1. The same letter or letters should be used in the next row plus an additional letter.
2. The letters may be rearranged to form a new word.
3. Each word should correspond to the given clue.

Follow the clues to fill in the word pyramid.

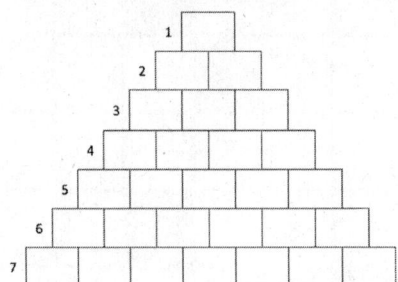

Clues
1. 13th letter of the alphabet.
2. Myself.
3. Adult male human beings.
4. A dug hole in the earth for extracting coal.
5. To cut up or grind.
6. Movie theatre.
7. 'Don't forget to put the clothes in the washing _____ (device) before you leave.'

Time taken: _____

Word Unscramble: Hidden Animals

Unscramble the animals that are hidden in the following words.

1. AFGFERI
2. RAZBE
3. PAEHLETN

PUZZLE 12: LOOPY LOOPS

Draw a single loop that passes through the centre of every white square, using only horizontal and vertical lines. The loop cannot pass through any square more than once, cannot cross itself or pass through any of the black squares.

Look at the example given below to get an idea of the completed puzzle.

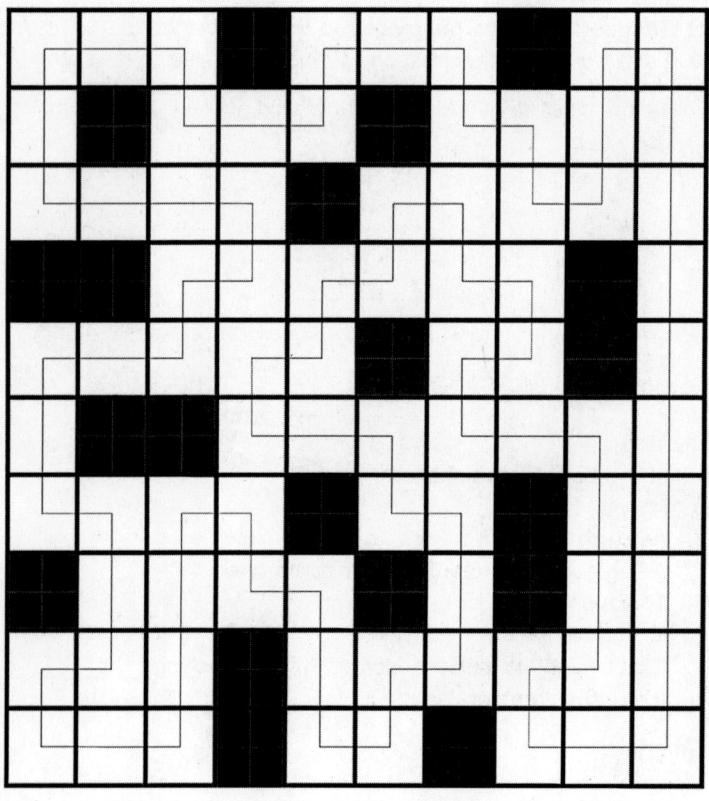

TIME LIMIT: 20 MINUTES

A)

B)

Time taken: _____

Riddle Me This

Sarah has four daughters. Each of her daughters has one brother. How many children does Sarah have?

PUZZLE 13: WHAT COMES NEXT?

Look at the sequences of tiles below and logically work out what answer should fit into the blank box at the end. Try to work out the plan, scheme or order behind every row and column of tiles. Choose your answer from options A to E. Each question may require a different kind of logic to solve it.

Looking at the example below, going row-wise, we can see that with each consecutive tile, an additional black block is added to the bottom. Going column-wise, we see that in the first, second and third column of tiles, each black block reduces by one from the right. Therefore, Option D would fit into the empty space.

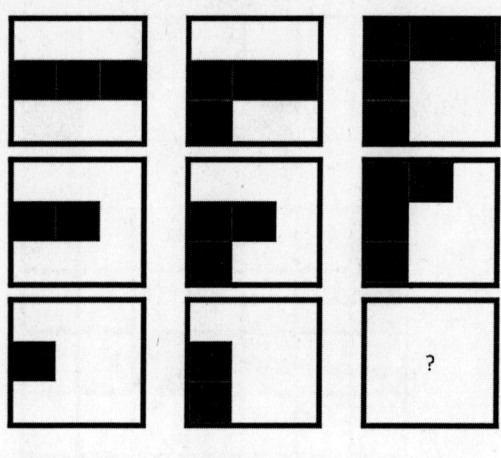

Options:

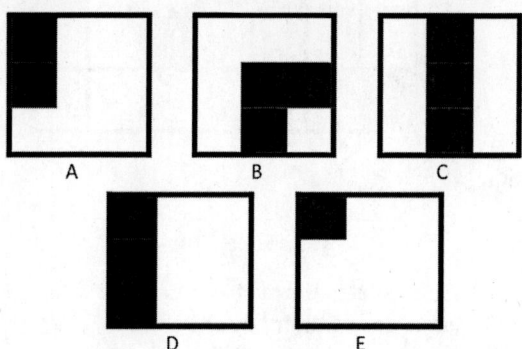

TIME LIMIT: 10 MINUTES

Exercise:

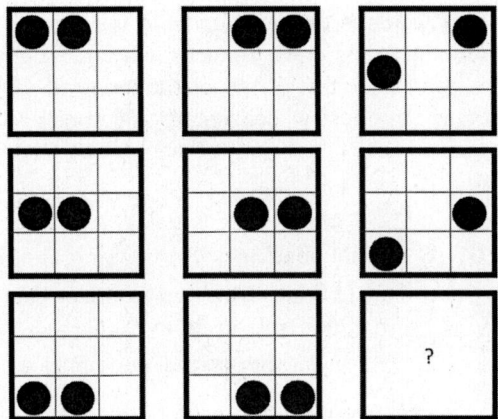

Options:

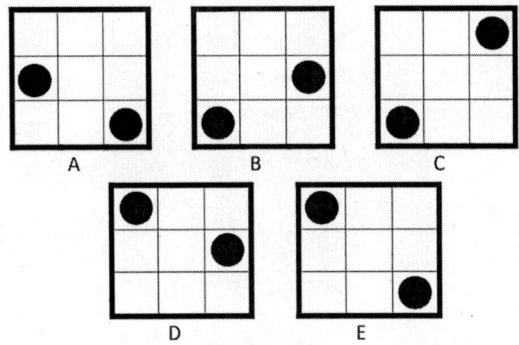

Time taken: _____

Brain Teaser: Add Word

Which single 5-letter word can be attached to the end of the following words to create three new words?

1. Club
2. Farm
3. Ware

__ __ __ __ __

PUZZLE 14: WORD SQUARES

TIME LIMIT: 10 MINUTES

Word squares consist of a set of words written in a grid in such a way that the same words can be read both horizontally and vertically. The number of words is generally equal to the number of letters in each word. All the words cross perfectly in a square arrangement.

You are given clues that correspond to the rows. All you need to do is write down the answer horizontally and vertically to complete the word square.

Example:

E	G	G	S	What hens lay
G	O	A	L	In football, if the ball is kicked into the net, it is said to be a _____
G	A	L	A	An event with special performances.
S	L	A	P	To hit with the palm of the hand.

Work out the word squares below:

A)

Highest and lowest value card in a deck of cards.

Feline house pet

Short for *et cetera*

B)

Newborn.

A region or part of a town.

Jack and the __ __ __ __ stalk.

Pull with a jerk.

Time taken: _____

Reasoning Puzzle

Five people A, B, C, D and E were eating chocolate. A finished before B but after C. D finished before E but after B. What was the order in which they all finished eating the chocolate?

PUZZLE 15: WORD CIRCLES

TIME LIMIT: 10 MINUTES

Given below are six-letter words arranged in circles. They are not jumbled. Find the correct word and write it down. The words can be read clockwise or counterclockwise.

1.
```
        O
    N       T
    N       C
        A
```
Answer: _____

2.
```
        I
    S       D
    N       E
        I
```
Answer: _____

3.
```
        E
    R       W
    D       A
        R
```
Answer: _____

4.
```
        O
    H       L
    W       L
        Y
```
Answer: _____

5.
```
        N
    L       U
    I       E
        K
```
Answer: _____

6.
```
        R
    E       F
    M       O
        R
```
Answer: _____

7.
```
        O
    M       D
    E       U
        L
```
Answer: _____

8.
```
        I
    G       S
    N       D
        E
```
Answer: _____

9.
```
        L
    L       E
    A       Y
        V
```
Answer: _____

10.
```
        V
    M       I
    I       C
        T
```
Answer: _____

Time taken: _____

PUZZLE 16: REVERSE MINESWEEPER

Reverse minesweeper is a puzzle that begins with all the answers revealed. You will need to place mines around the number squares. The number of mines around a number square corresponds to the number of the square. For example, if the number is 2, it indicates that there are two mines in the immediate squares that surround it.

Rules
1. Place a mine into the empty squares that surround each number, including diagonally adjacent squares. You can either draw a mine or shade the cell to represent the mine.
2. The number of mines around a number needs to correspond to the value of the number.

Hints
1. There may be blank squares as well. Mark these off with an X so that you don't get confused.
2. Start with a square that you know for sure is a mine.

Look at the example given below to get an idea of the completed puzzle.

2	●	2		0			1	1
2	●	2			1	1	2	●
	1		0		1	●	3	2
	0				1	1	2	●
			1	1	1		1	1
	0		2	●	2			0
1	1		2	●	4	2	1	
●	1		1	2	●	●	1	
1	1	0		1	2	2	1	

TIME LIMIT: 10 MINUTES

A) Place 11 mines in the puzzle below.

1		3	2		0
	3				
2			4		2
3					3
	3	2			3
		1	2		2

B) Place 11 mines in the puzzle below.

	1		0	1	1	1
1						2
	3			4		
	2	4				1
3					0	
		2		2		
2	2		1		1	0

Time taken: _____

Riddle Me This

A man walked outside in a heavy rainstorm for twenty minutes without getting a single hair on his head wet. He didn't wear a hat, carry an umbrella, or hold anything over his head. His clothes got soaking wet though. How could this happen?

PUZZLE 17: MATCHING SHAPES   TIME LIMIT: 10 MINUTES

This puzzle is very simple. Draw lines to match each identical shape. The lines must not cross each other or touch each other. There must never be more than one connecting line in any square. All lines have to be horizontal or vertical lines only. No diagonal lines are allowed. Look at the example given below to get an idea of the completed puzzle.

Connect the identical shapes in the following puzzle.

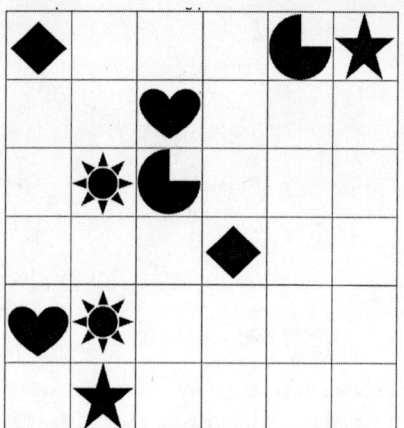

Time taken: _____

PUZZLE 18: TANGRAM

TIME LIMIT: 10 MINUTES

Using all seven tangram shapes from the beginning of the book, make the figure of the dancing man below. You can cut out the shapes from the book, trace the shapes on a different sheet of paper and cut them out, or use Tangram blocks, if you have them.

Rules
1. All seven pieces must be used.
2. All seven pieces must touch each other.
3. None of the pieces should overlap.

Time taken: _____

Brain Teaser: Add Word

Which single 3-letter word can be attached to the beginning of the following words to create three new words?

___ ___ ___ {
    1. Burn
    2. Spot
    3. Beam

PUZZLE 19: DIVIDING SHAPES

Divide the following figure into equal parts by drawing along the lines of the inner squares.

Rules
1. Each of the divided shapes should be identical to each other.
2. There should be no added or left out squares.
3. If all divided parts are rotated to face the same direction, they should all be exactly the same size and look exactly alike.

Hint
Count the squares inside the figure and divide the total by the total required. This will give you an idea of how many squares are needed inside the figure.

In the following example, the figure needs to be divided by **four** equal parts.

Answer:

TIME LIMIT: 10 MINUTES

Divide this square into **five** equal parts.

Time taken: _____

Bonus Puzzle: Letter Mash

C	N	F	D
K	A	J	E
I	O	G	H
L	B	P	M

Which letter is just below the letter that is immediately to the right of the letter that is three places above the letter that is two places to the left of the letter P?

Hint: Start from the end of the question and work backwards.

PUZZLE 20: CODE DECODE   TIME LIMIT: 20 MINUTES

Coded messages are one of the earliest forms of sending secret messages to people. The Caesar Cipher is one of the earliest known coded messages that date back to 100 BC! It was used by Julius Caesar to send secret messages to his Generals. These messages could only be decoded by the Generals and nobody else since they had the key to deciphering them.

Caesar's magic number was 3, which means that each letter was shifted by 3 places on the alphabet. So, A becomes D, B becomes E, and so on. When you reach the end of the alphabet, it would start over from A; so, X becomes A, Y becomes B and Z becomes C.

Given below are some codes that need to be decoded. The letters are shifted by 1, 3 or 5 spaces, either to the right or left of the coded letters given. Following the clues, try to decipher these common proverbs.

A) Q S B D U J D F   N B L F T   Q F S G F D U

Clues: 1. Two words begin with the letter P.
2. The letter E appears in all three words.
3. The letter C appears three times.

B) E H J J D U V   F D Q' W   E H   F K R R V H U V

Clues: 1. Two words begin with the letter B.
2. There are two Os that appear consecutively.
3. There are two Ss in one word.

C) V N   T J P   N J R,   N J   N C V G G   T J P   M Z V K

Clues: 1. The word 'YOU' is repeated twice.
2. Three words begin with the letter S.
3. There are two Ls that appear consecutively.

Time taken: _____

Fun Activity: Invisible Ink

Would you like to send secret messages to your friends that nobody else can read? Here's the recipe for invisible ink. Simply add a few drops of water to some lemon juice. Now dip a cotton bud into the mixture and write your secret message on a piece of paper with it. Wait for the paper to dry. The juice now becomes invisible. Pass the paper to your friend and ask them to heat it up by keeping it close to a light bulb. Voila! The message appears!

PUZZLE 21: COUNTING CUBES   TIME LIMIT: 5 MINUTES

Count the cubes in the image below. Keep in mind that this image is in 3D and there may be some cubes that you cannot see.

Hint: Don't forget to count the cubes that are hidden behind or beneath the cubes that you can see. For example, in the image below, there is one hidden cube at the back on the right. This makes a total of 7 cubes.

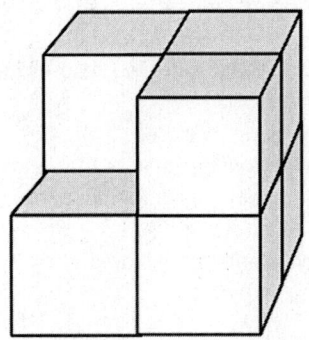

How many cubes are present in the image below?

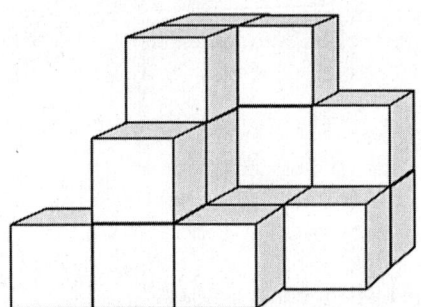

Time taken: _____

Riddle Me This

I have a face but no eyes,
Hands but no arms.
What am I?

PUZZLE 22: CROSSWORD FARM

Given below are clues that relate to animals, birds, buildings, plants and farming components. Solve the clues to complete the crossword puzzle on the next page.

Across
2. A __ __ __ __ of cattle.
7. What we get from (clue) 11 across.
8. An animal that neighs.
9. The part of the animal where we get 7 across.
11. Animal that moos.
12. Usually a house pet but can also help in herding sheep.
14. Man who owns a farm.
17. Tall tower where grain is stored.
18. A railing, typically of wood or wire that encloses the whole farm.
20. Grass grown as grain, used for flour, bread, and cattle fodder (starts with the letter R).
21. Medium in which plants are planted.
22. Baby pig.
23. Baby of (clue) 3 down.
28. What is used to scare off birds.
29. Mid-sized bird (starts with the letter Q).

Down
1. A farming tool (starts with the letter P).
2. Where bees live.
3. Bird that quacks.
4. Bird that clucks.
5. Something that gets bigger is said to __ __ __ __.
6. Something that is added to 21 across to help plants grow.
7. Large open areas where 11 across may graze in.
10. Past tense of dig.
13. A large shed where cattle can live.
15. Baby of 8 across.
16. Another word for grime or dust (starts with the letter D).
18. An area of open land that may be planted with crops. Similar to (clue) 7 down.
19. Baby of (clue) 4 down.
21. Part of a plant that you sow in (clue) 21 across (plural).
24. Where (clue) 4 down lives.
25. This animal's baby is called a kid.

26. A _ _ _ _ of hay.
27. Another name for a pigsty is a pig___ ___ ___.

TIME LIMIT: 20 MINUTES

Time taken: _____

Bonus Puzzle: Rebus Puzzle

A Rebus puzzle is a picture representation of a common word, saying or phrase. For example, /R/E/A/D/I/N/G/ could be interpreted as 'Reading between the lines'. Try and solve the following Rebus puzzles.

1.	2.	3.	4.
STAND ——— TRY 2	TRAVEL ——— CCCCCCCC	WHAT (rotated)	MUST (rotated)	GIVE GET GIVE GET GIVE GET GIVE GET

PUZZLE 23: HASHI

This puzzle is called hashi or bridges. It is a logic puzzle with simple rules. All you have to do is to connect all the islands with bridges.

Rules
1. The number of bridges coming in and going out from each island needs to be the same as the number inside the island.
2. You can only draw horizontal and vertical lines to connect islands. No diagonal lines are allowed.
3. Bridges cannot cut across each other or any of the islands.
4. Draw one line to represent one bridge.
5. There cannot be more than two bridges for each pair of islands (although there can be more bridges leading away from the island to a different island). The total number of bridges per island can be anywhere from one to eight, depending on the number inside the island.
6. All islands must be connected so that if you start at one island, you should be able to travel to every other island using the bridges.

Hint
Start with an island where you know for sure which direction the bridges go. For example, in the image below, there cannot be any horizontal bridges for the number 2 on the left column. Therefore, you know for sure that both bridges will have to connect to the number 5 above it. Look at the example given below to get an idea of the completed puzzle.

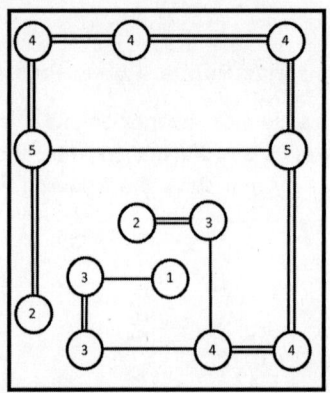

TIME LIMIT: 20 MINUTES

Connect all islands with bridges.

A) **Hint:** Start with island 1 in the fifth row.

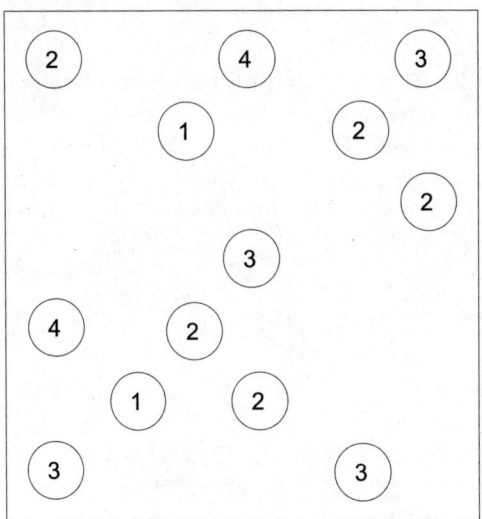

B) **Hint:** Start with the corner island 4 in the last row.

Time taken: _____

PUZZLE 24: LETTER SLIDES   TIME LIMIT: 10 MINUTES

Letter slides are formed by starting at one letter and sliding your way to a connecting letter to form a word. Solve the clues below to find words.

Rules
1. Words can be formed only by sliding from one letter to another letter that is either above, below, to the left, right or diagonal to the previous letter. You cannot skip letters to reach another letter.
2. You cannot use the same letter more than once in any word.

B	A	K	I
R	E	G	N

Clues
A) When a cake is in the oven, it is said to be ___ ___ ___ ___ ___ ___. (6 letters)
B) Queen's husband ___ ___ ___ ___. (4 letters)
C) Garden tool used to collect fallen leaves ___ ___ ___ ___. (4 letters)
D) 'I ___ ___ ___ your pardon?' (3 letters)
E) When you start something, you are said to ___ ___ ___ ___ ___ it. (5 letters)
F) Something that you can carry around and holds all your things ___ ___ ___. (3 letters)
G) A dirty cloth ___ ___ ___. (3 letters)
H) The gift of the ___ ___ ___ (someone who can talk fluently) (3 letters)
I) An athletic sports brand. Also the name of the Goddess of Victory in Greek mythology. ___ ___ ___ ___ (4 letters)
J) Can you find the 8 letter word that uses all the letter slides? Start with the letter B.

Time taken: _____

PUZZLE 25: MATH WHIZ   TIME LIMIT: 10 MINUTES

Solve the following mathematical links to get your final answer. Try to solve them in your head without writing anything down or using a calculator. Just follow the links downwards and solve the mathematical instructions given in each link. Once you have the answer, move to the next link.

For example, when we look at Question A, we start with the number 20, and then divide it by 4. Add the number 5 to the answer. Once you get the answer, move to the link below and subtract the number 7 from it. You will then need to multiply that number by 6, and so on. Write your answer in the last blank link.

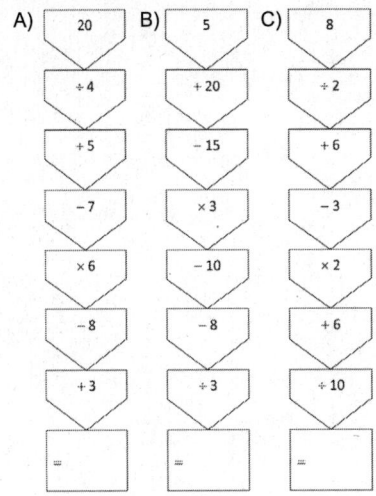

Time taken: _____

Fun fact

Language skills get better as you grow older but your mathematical abilities may decline if you don't exercise your brain. Using maths (without a calculator) in your daily life will help keep your brain sharp. You could try to calculate the cost of your bill at a restaurant before you receive your cheque, measure out ingredients accurately in a recipe, try to calculate the discount on an item during a sale, figure out the distance and time it would take to reach a destination while you're travelling, etc.

EASY PUZZLES

PUZZLE 26: MAZE AMAZE   TIME LIMIT: 10 MINUTES

Time taken: _____

Fun Fact

Enigmatology is the study and science of puzzles of any kind—mathematical, word and logic puzzles!

PUZZLE 27: WORD LADDERS

A word ladder is a sequence of words formed by just changing one letter at a time.

Rules
1. The first and last words are given. Working your way up or down the ladder, change only *one* letter in each word to get the next word—eventually ending with the final word.
2. All words have to be real words and not made-up words.
3. All words need to have the same number of letters as the first and last words. You cannot make the words longer or shorter.
4. The number of rungs in the ladder indicates how many words are needed to make the final word. In both examples 1 and 2, there are four words that are needed to make BOOK to READ and BATH to TUBS respectively.

Look at the examples given below to get an idea of how to solve this puzzle.

Example 1: Change BOOK to READ

B	O	O	K
B	O	O	T
B	O	A	T
B	E	A	T
B	E	A	D
R	E	A	D

Example 2: Change BATH to TUBS

B	A	T	H
B	A	T	S
C	A	T	S
C	U	T	S
C	U	B	S
T	U	B	S

TIME LIMIT: 10 MINUTES

A) Help the FOOT kick the BALL. Some clues are given to help you.

F	O	O	T
B	A	L	L

A type of shoe that covers the ankles.

Something that helps you lock a door.

Something that helps you tighten your pants.

Something that rings to signal that school is over.

B) Make FIRE into HEAT in four steps.

F	I	R	E
H	E	A	T

Another word for 'to rent.'

In *this* place.

A group of cattle.

Where you would wear a hat.

Time taken: _____

Bonus Game: Assembling a Word Square

Arrange the tiles to form a 4x4 square such that the words read the same across and down. Look at Puzzles 14, 39, 64 and 89 to get an idea of what word squares are.

	T			N	D		N					M	I
T	A		E	A		D	A		E	A		I	D

PUZZLE 28: DOMINO TWIST

Places the dominoes in their correct places.

Rules
1. Place the eight dominoes in the shaded spaces provided.
2. Each domino piece can be rotated to fit into the space.
3. The domino piece that you place must match the piece already provided. For example, if the edge piece has five dots on it, the domino that you place next to it also needs to have five dots.

Hint
1. If you have domino pieces at home, you can use those to help you solve this puzzle.
2. You can trace out the eight domino pieces on a sheet of paper, cut them out and then place them on the puzzle. This makes it easier to rotate the pieces to see where they may fit.
3. Start with the domino that you know will definitely fit into a specific place.

Look at the example below to see how to match the dominoes.

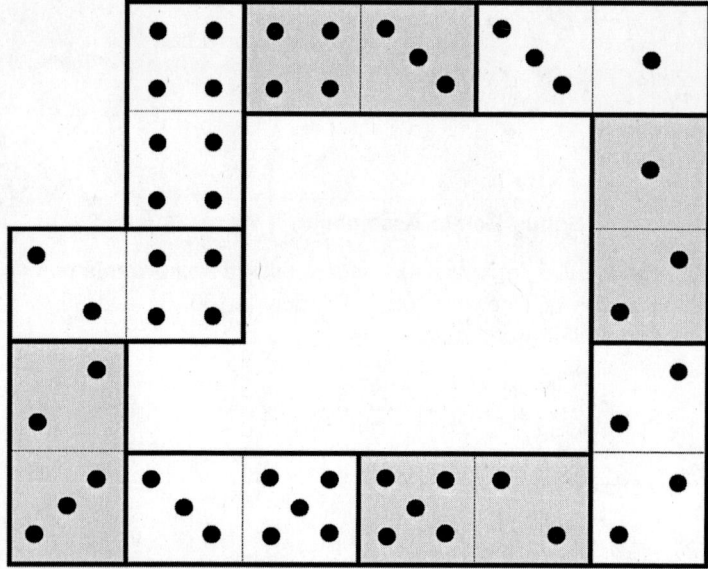

TIME LIMIT: 10 MINUTES

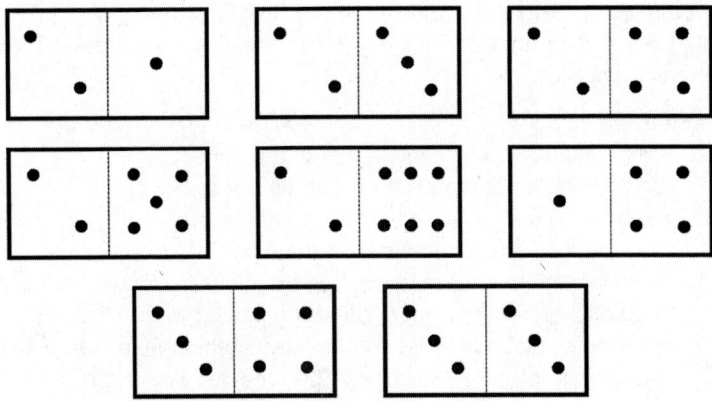

Place the dominoes above in the figure below.

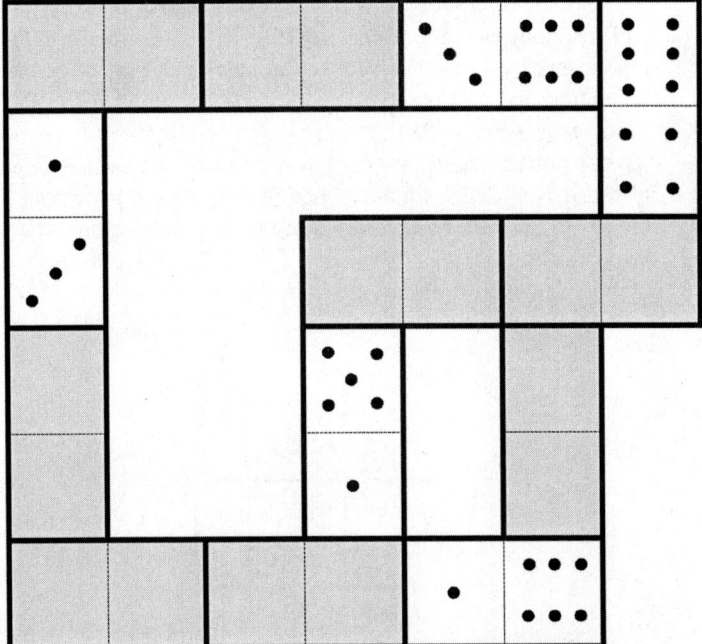

Time taken: _____

PUZZLE 29: MINI SUDOKU

Given below is a mini Sudoku puzzle that involves a 6x6 grid of squares divided into 3x2 blocks. Fill in the blank squares with the correct numbers.

Rules
1. Every square should contain just one number.
2. Only the numbers from 1 to 6 can be used.
3. Each 3x2 block must contain all numbers from 1 to 6. None of the numbers can be repeated in the block.
4. Each vertical column must contain the numbers from 1 to 6 only once. None of the numbers can be repeated in the column.
5. Each horizontal row must contain the numbers from 1 to 6 only once. None of the numbers can be repeated in the rows.

Hint
1. When you start the Sudoku puzzle, some squares will already be filled with numbers. Use those numbers as clues for blank squares.
2. Start by identifying the blank squares that give you a definite answer. Once you do this, you will be able to deduce other blank squares around that number.
3. Some blank squares may initially look like they may hold more than one possible number. Pencil in all possible numbers and move on to the next blank square. Once you figure out a number for certain, go back to the squares that have more than one answer and erase that number from that square. This will help eliminate numbers until you arrive at just one answer.

Example:

4	6	2	3	5	1
3	1	5	2	6	4
5	2	6	1	4	3
1	3	4	5	2	6
2	4	3	6	1	5
6	5	1	4	3	2

TIME LIMIT: 10 MINUTES

A)

3	5	6		4	2
	2				3
		4		1	5
1	6	5	2	3	
5			4		
6			3	5	1

B)

	3	1	4	5	
4	5		1		2
	6		2		3
1		3		4	5
3		2		6	
	4		3	2	1

Time taken: _____

Riddle Me This

Take away my first letter, I sound the same. Take away my last letter, I still sound the same. Take away my middle letter, I still sound the same. I am a five letter word. What am I?

PUZZLE 30: COIN BOARD

Look at the 6x6 grid on the next page. Place two coins on each row so that each row, column and the two main diagonals contain only two coins.

Rules
1. You can place only one coin on a square.
2. Each row, column and main diagonal must contain only two coins.

Hint
1. You can use real coins for this puzzle or simply shade in the squares on which you would place a coin. You need 12 coins.
2. Start at the centre and work your way outwards.

Look at the example given below to get an idea of the completed puzzle.

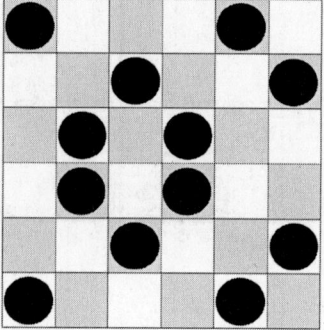

Bonus Game: Anagrams

An anagram is a word that can be formed by rearranging the letters of another word. For example, LOOPED is an anagram of POODLE. Find the anagram for the words that are in capital letters.
1. She ___ ___ ___ ___ every time she has a meeting with the BOSS.
2. I took NOTE of her ___ ___ ___ ___ of voice.
3. They invited us to TEA to ___ ___ ___ some buttered scones.
4. HOW did they get in? ___ ___ ___ do you think stole the painting?
5. He tried to ___ ___ ___ ___ the VASE from falling and breaking.

TIME LIMIT: 10 MINUTES

Solve the puzzles below. Four coins are already placed to help you get started.

A)

B)

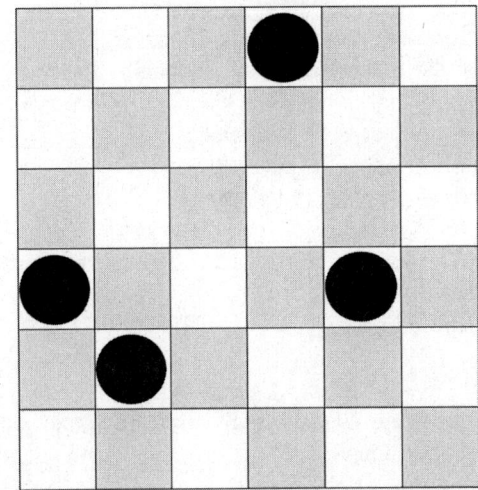

Time taken: _____

PUZZLE 31: WORD SWIRL
TIME LIMIT: 10 MINUTES

How many words of four or more letters can you make from the following word swirl?

Rules
1. Follow the clues below to find the word.
2. Each word must have the centre letter (D) in it.
3. All words have to be real words and not made up.

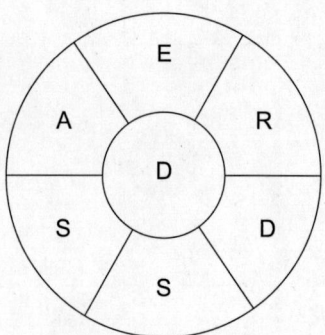

Clues
1. A 3-letter word for Father. (3 letters)
2. Short form of advertisements. (3 letters)
3. One of the primary colours. (3 letters)
4. Something that is not alive anymore. (4 letters)
5. This is the best book I've ever ___ ___ ___ ___. (4 letters)
6. Opposite of happy. (3 letters)
7. An item of clothing. (5 letters)
8. Truth or ___ ___ ___ ___. (4 letters)
9. A small venomous snake with a dark zigzag pattern on its back. (5 letters)
10. More sad (6 letters)

Bonus
Can you guess the 7-letter word? (**Hint:** It's something to do with the location of your house.)

Time taken: _____

PUZZLE 32: FOLDING CUBES   TIME LIMIT: 10 MINUTES

How many of the following cube nets can form three-dimensional cubes when they are folded?

Rules
1. Imagine that each shape is folded along its lines. You will have to manipulate the shapes in your mind and see which cube nets form cubes. If you find it hard to do this, trace or draw the shapes on a separate piece of paper and physically fold them on their lines to see if it makes a cube.
2. There should not be any overlapping flaps.

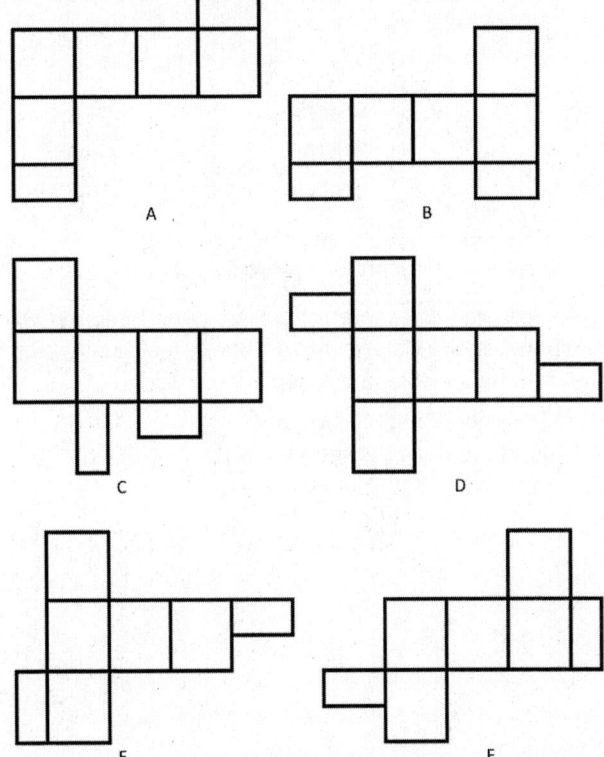

Time taken: _____

PUZZLE 33: WORD SEARCH– O

Find and circle the following words in the word search puzzle on the next page. All words begin with the letter O. The words can be found horizontally, vertically or diagonally, in any direction (back to front or bottom to top). There are 30 words to find in 30 minutes so try and find all the words as quickly as possible!

- Overhead
- Opposite
- Occasion
- Outdoors
- Onboard
- Octopus
- Outcast
- Office
- Obtuse
- Outwit
- Oodles
- Outbox
- Oblong
- Octave
- Offend
- Origami
- Online
- Oafish
- Orient
- Orphan
- Ozone
- Optic
- Overcame
- Obligate
- Oxidize
- Oyster
- Oddball
- Ornate
- Octane
- Opener

Bonus: Above/Below

Using the following clues, place the letters A to I into the grid below. **Hint:** 'Above/below' refers to two letters in the same column. Left/right refers to two letters in the same row.

a) C is below G and above E
b) D is above A and to the right of F
c) F is above I and to the left of D
d) A is above H and to the right of I
e) H is to the right of B and to the left of E.

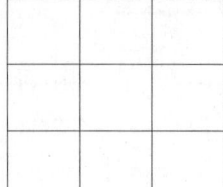

TIME LIMIT: 30 MINUTES

				O	V	E	R	H	E	A	D					
			O	Q	C	R	D	O	P	U	T	P	E	Z		
		L	Y	E	C	I	F	F	O	K	G	P	H	N	X	
	D	J	S	X	A	Q	V	B	O	R	P	H	A	N	A	M
V	O	B	T	U	S	E	M	L	P	M	K	G	V	B	G	T	W
F	G	H	E	W	I	D	Q	Z	X	V	X	Z	Q	M	N	B	C
P	M	N	C	R	V	O	U	T	D	O	O	R	S	L	K	O	L	G	O
D	R	F	H	G	Q	N	W	Z	V	B	C	C	E	D	J	N	J	K	B
L	P	B	N	M	D	V	B					L	T	V	K	L	N	M	L
D	N	E	F	F	O	B						A	A	H	I	D	V	O
O	K	L	R	Z	N	O						G	B	V	N	G	Q	N
V	T	M	O	N	G	X						I	D	G	E	V	Q	G
E	B	N	R	G	B	I						L	L	A	B	D	D	O
R	E	R	I	V	W	D						B	V	B	V	F	W	A
C	B	V	G	C	K	I						O	F	H	O	F	R	F
A	Y	T	A	M	L	Z						G	F	Q	R	X	Z	I
M	B	Y	M	D	D	E						D	R	S	I	W	C	S
E	T	B	I	Q	Z	M	H				O	O	D	L	E	S	V	H
G	J	I	V	Q	P	O	P	E	N	E	R	U	U	W	Q	N	Z	X	V
B	V	R	W	E	B	D	V	D	X	W	V	T	T	V	Z	T	B	P	J
	P	G	T	T	V	R	V	C	W	G	H	C	B	J	F	R	W	Z
	G	V	C	A	U	A	P	H	J	K	L	A	O	P	T	I	C	K
		J	P	N	V	O	C	T	O	P	U	S	X	B	Q	Z	X
			G	R	M	B	P	Q	W	Z	X	T	B	V	Y	R
				O	Q	N	Z	P	L	K	B	M	G	T	H
					O	P	P	O	S	I	T	E

Time taken: _____

Fun Fact

The first jigsaw puzzle was created in 1767 when John Spilsbury, an English cartographer (map-maker), chopped up a wooden map of Britain and challenged the public to reassemble it. He called it a 'dissected puzzle.'

PUZZLE 34: SLITHERLINKS

The objective of this puzzle is to use the numbers inside the squares as guides to help you draw horizontal or vertical 'fences' around the entire puzzle to form a simple loop, with no open ends. The numbers 1, 2 and 3 inside the squares represent the number of fences or loops around that particular number.

Rules
1. The fence or loop has to be a single continuous line throughout the puzzle. All line segments must be connected.
2. The loop cannot touch or cross itself at any point. It also cannot be left open at any point.
3. The number of fences around a particular number should correspond to that number. For example, if the number is 2, then only two fences can be drawn around that number, either to the left, right, top or bottom of the number.
4. If there is no number in a square, you can draw any number of lines surrounding that square in order to connect the loop to the numbered squares.

Hints
1. If the number of fences surrounding a square correspond to the number in the square, all other possible horizontal and vertical lines surrounding that square can be eliminated.
2. Start with a number which points to a definite fence. For example, if there is a 3 in the corner, you know for sure that the two outside edges need to be drawn. That leaves only the two inside edges, which can be deduced using the other numbers surrounding it.

Example:

3	2	2		1	1	
	1		1			2
	3		1		3	
3					1	1
		3				
	3	2	1		1	2

TIME LIMIT: 20 MINUTES

A)

3					3
		1	1		
1	3	2			3
3			2	2	2
		3			
	1				2

B)

3		1	3				
	2			3	2		2
2	1	2	2	2	1	2	
	2				3	1	2
3	1	3				1	
	2	2	1		1	1	2
2		2	3			3	
				3	2		2

Time taken: _____

> **Riddle Me This**
>
> The day before two days after the day before tomorrow is Saturday. What day is it today?

PUZZLE 35: MYTHICAL CREATURES REVERSE CROSSWORD
TIME LIMIT: 10 MINUTES

In reverse crossword, all the answers are already given; you will just need to place each answer in its correct slot. This puzzle requires pure logic to solve and does not involve any guess work. Fit all the mythical creatures into their correct boxes.

11-letter words
Leprechauns

8-letter words
Adroanzi
Dirawong
Minotaur
Unicorns

7-letter words
Cyclops
Mermaid
Phoenix

6-letter words
Drakon
Gnomes
Goblin
Kumiho
Sphinx
Oni

5-letter words
Amala
Hydra
Ogres
Troll
Ghoul

4-letter words
Faun
Lynx

3-letter words
Imp

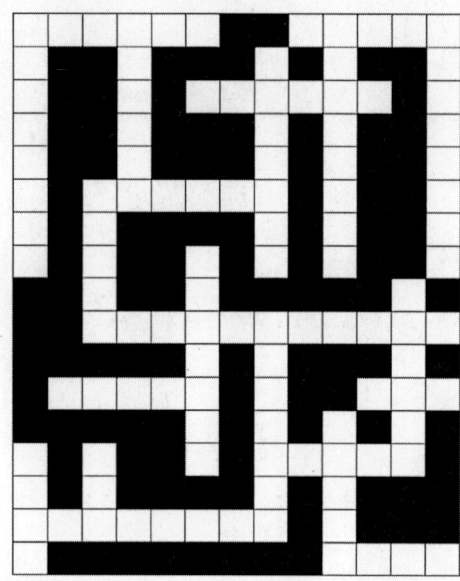

Time taken: _____

PUZZLE 36: WORD PYRAMID   TIME LIMIT: 10 MINUTES

Beginning at the top, move towards the bottom seven-letter word by adding a letter at each step. Solve each clue and write the answer in each corresponding row.

Rules
1. The same letter or letters should be used in the next row plus an additional letter.
2. The letters may be rearranged to form a new word.
3. Each word should correspond to the given clue.

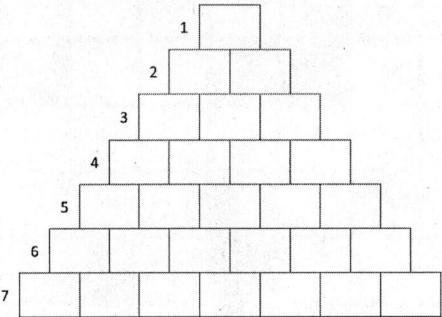

Clues
1. First letter of the alphabet.
2. Short form for agriculture.
3. To grow old.
4. Donated.
5. A burial place.
6. The destructive effects of something.
7. A standard or level which is considered to be typical or usual. E.g.: He wasn't a great basketball player, he was just _____.

Time taken: _____

Logical thinking: Analogies

Look at the relationship between the first pair of words and then apply the same logic to the next pair of words. Tick the option.
Frame is to picture as:
A) criminal is to gang   B) binding is to book
C) carpenter is to artist   D) nail is to hammer

PUZZLE 37: LOOPY LOOPS

Draw a single loop that passes through the centre of every white square, using only horizontal and vertical lines. The loop cannot pass through any square more than once, cannot cross itself or pass through any of the black squares.

Look at the example given below to get an idea of the completed puzzle.

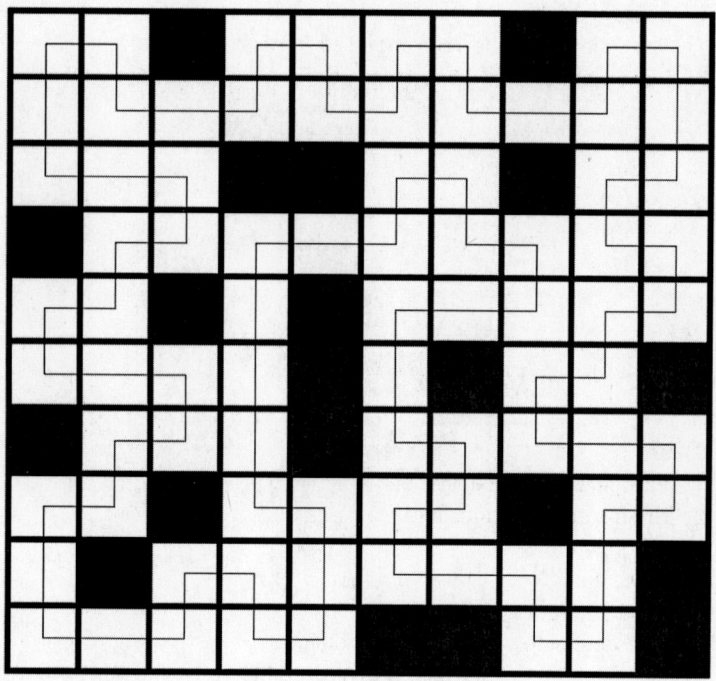

TIME LIMIT: 20 MINUTES

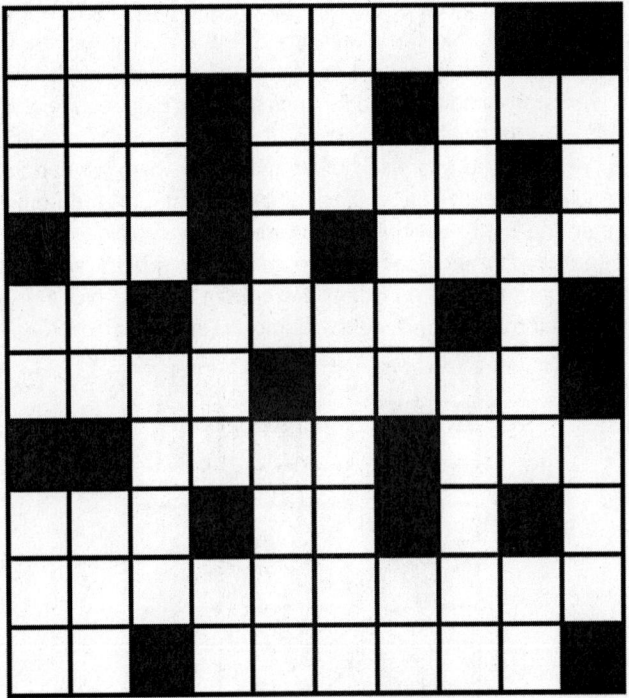

Time taken: _____

Bonus Puzzle: Rebus Puzzle

A Rebus puzzle is a picture representation of a common word, saying or phrase. For example, /R/E/A/D/I/N/G/ could be interpreted as 'Reading between the lines'. Try and solve the following Rebus puzzles.

1.	2.	3.	4.
GSGE	→SECRET	I FELL	
EGSG	SECRET	I FELL	
GGSE	SECRET	I FELL	JACK
SGEG		I FELL	
		I FELL	
		I FELL	

PUZZLE 38: WHAT COMES NEXT?

Look at the sequences of the tiles below and logically work out what answer should fit into the blank box at the end. Try to work out the plan, scheme or order behind every row and column of tiles. Choose your answer from options A to E. Each question may require a different kind of logic to solve.

Looking at the example below, going row-wise, we can see that with each consecutive tile, a black square is first removed from the left and then the right, leaving only the middle tiles. Going column-wise, we see that with each consecutive column, one black square is first removed from the top and then the bottom, leaving only the middle tiles. Therefore, Option A would fit into the empty space.

Options:

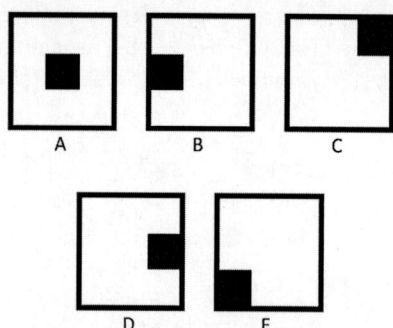

TIME LIMIT: 10 MINUTES

Find the missing tile from Options A to E.

Options:

Time taken: _____

Bonus Game: Odd One Out

Find the odd word out of the following words.

Label	Museum	Wow	Swims
Comic	Bathtub	Sobs	Taunt
Yummy	Mummy	Drooled	Health
Throat	Teapot	Fluff	Lawful

PUZZLE 39: WORD SQUARES   TIME LIMIT: 10 MINUTES

Word square consists of a set of words written in a grid in such a way that the same words can be read both horizontally and vertically. The number of words is generally equal to the number of letters in each word. All the words cross perfectly in a square arrangement.

You are given clues that correspond to the rows. All you need to do is write down the answer horizontally and vertically to complete the Word Square.

Example:

S	H	O	W
H	I	K	E
O	K	R	A
W	E	A	R

'Welcome home, let me ___ ___ ___ ___ you around.'

A trek or long walk.

A vegetable, commonly called 'ladies' fingers'.

'You can ___ ___ ___ ___ (put on) my hat.'

Work out the Word Squares below:

A)

Leave out or remove.

Past tense of make.

Sudden thought as to what to do.

Group of people working together.

B)

What you do to make the candles go out on the birthday cake.

Opposite of hate.

Finished.

Past tense of 'are'.

Time taken: _____

PUZZLE 40: WORD CIRCLES

TIME LIMIT: 10 MINUTES

Given below are seven-letter words arranged in circles. They are not jumbled. Find the correct word and write it down. The words can be read clockwise or counterclockwise.

1.
```
      R
   E     Y
   L     G
     L A
```
Answer: _____

2.
```
      I
   S     F
   H     G
     I N
```
Answer: _____

3.
```
      I
   N     R
   T     P
     E R
```
Answer: _____

4.
```
      E
   W     L
   E     C
     M O
```
Answer: _____

5.
```
      C
   I     A
   S     L
     U M
```
Answer: _____

Time taken: _____

6.
```
      J
   O     Y
   U     E
     R N
```
Answer: _____

7.
```
      M
   E     E
   S     G
     S A
```
Answer: _____

8.
```
      E
   D     I
   S     D
     T U
```
Answer: _____

9.
```
      I
   N     D
   G     A
     R E
```
Answer: _____

10.
```
      C
   S     H
   S     O
     L O
```
Answer: _____

PUZZLE 41: REVERSE MINESWEEPER

Reverse minesweeper is a puzzle that begins with all the answers revealed. You will need to place mines around the number squares. The number of mines around a number square corresponds to the number of the square. For example, if the number is 2, it indicates that there are two mines in the immediate squares that surround it.

Rules
1. Place a mine into the empty squares that surround each number, including diagonally adjacent squares. You can either draw a mine or shade the cell to represent the mine.
2. The number of mines around a number needs to correspond to the value of the number.

Hints
1. There may be blank squares as well. Mark these off with an X so that you don't get confused.
2. Start with a square that you know for sure is a mine.

Look at the example given below to get an idea of the completed puzzle.

0				1	●	1		0
	1	1	1	1	1	1	1	1
1	2	●	1				1	●
2	●	3	1	1	1	1	2	2
2	●	2		1	●	1	1	●
1	2	3	2	2	1	1	1	1
	1	●	●	2	1	1		
	1	2	2	2	●	1	0	
	0			1	1	1		

TIME LIMIT: 10 MINUTES

A) Place 9 mines in the puzzle below.

1		1		2	
		2	1		
3			1	2	2
		2	1	2	
2	2	1			
	1		2		3

B) Place 13 mines in the puzzle below.

3		2		1	3	
		2			4	
	2	1		2		
	2	1	1		2	2
	2			1	1	
1	2	3		2		2
	0					

Time taken: _____

> **Riddle Me This**
>
> I am tomorrow's yesterday and yesterday's tomorrow. What day am I?

PUZZLE 42: MATCHING SHAPES   TIME LIMIT: 10 MINUTES

Draw lines to match each identical shape. The lines must not cross each other or touch each other. There must never be more than one connecting line in any square. All lines have to be horizontal or vertical lines only. No diagonal lines are allowed. Look at the example given below to get an idea of the completed puzzle.

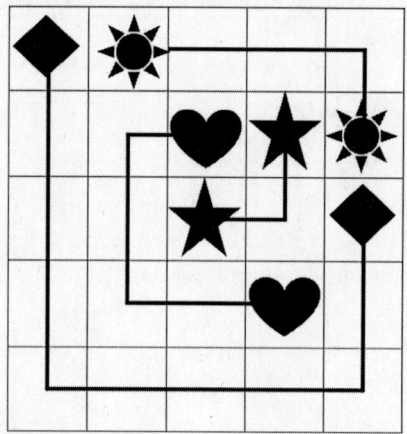

Connect the identical shapes in the following puzzle.

Time taken: _____

PUZZLE 43: TANGRAM   TIME LIMIT: 10 MINUTES

Using all seven tangram shapes from the beginning of the book, make the figure of the swan below. You can cut out the shapes from the book, trace the shapes on a different sheet of paper and cut them out, or use Tangram blocks, if you have them.

Rules
1. All seven pieces must be used.
2. All seven pieces must touch each other.
3. None of the pieces should overlap.

Time taken: _____

Bonus Game: Anagrams

An anagram is a word that can be formed by rearranging the letters of another word. For example, LOOPED is an anagram of POODLE. Find the anagram for the words that are capital letters.

1. The WOLF was quietly watching the river ___ ___ ___ ___.
2. Lisa poked the SNAIL with her ___ ___ ___ ___ ___.
3. There was a LUMP in the ___ ___ ___ ___ that she was eating.
4. Every year when it rains, the WELLS ___ ___ ___ ___ ___ up with water.
5. Mom turned off the STOVE to watch the elections to see which candidate got the most ___ ___ ___ ___ ___.

PUZZLE 44: DIVIDING SHAPES

Divide the following figure into equal parts by drawing along the lines of the inner squares.

Rules
1. Each of the divided shapes should be identical to each other.
2. There should be no added or left out squares.
3. If all divided parts are rotated to face the same direction, they should all be exactly the same size and should look exactly alike.

Hint
Count the squares inside the figure and divide the total by the total required. This will give you an idea of how many squares are needed inside the figure.

In the following example, the figure needs to be divided by **three** equal parts.

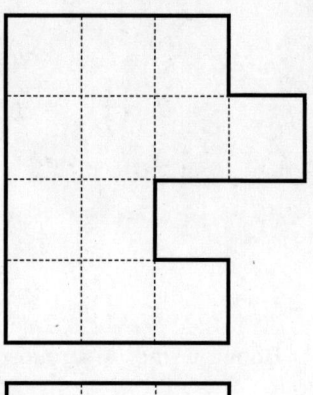

Answer:

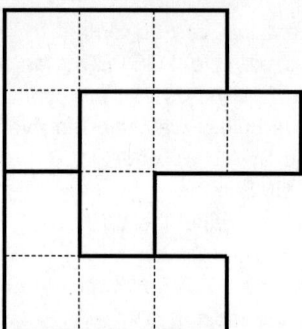

TIME LIMIT: 10 MINUTES

A) Divide the following shape into **five** equal parts, each part being identical.

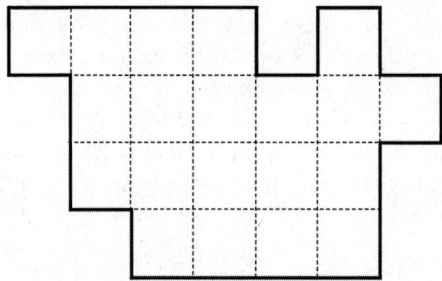

B) Divide the following shape into **six** equal parts, each part being identical.

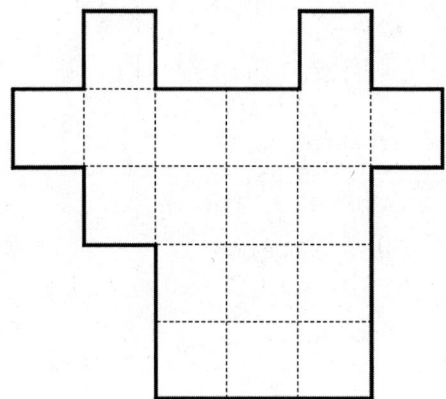

Time taken: _____

Bonus Game: Word Finder

Find at least **ten** 4-letter words in the word scramble below. Can you also find two words that use up all the 8 letters?

| S | I | D | F | E | H | N | I |

PUZZLE 45: CODE DECODE

TIME LIMIT: 20 MINUTES

You are already familiar with the Caesar Cipher from Puzzle 20 where you had to substitute a letter of the alphabet with other letters. This puzzle uses another substitution cipher called the Polybius Cipher, which is named after a Greek historian named Polybius (200-118 BC). This cipher substitutes numbers for letters in numeric order. So, since A is the first letter of the alphabet, the number assigned to A is 1; since B is the second letter, the number that is assigned to B is 2 and so on till you reach Z, which is number 26. All you have to do is to substitute the numbers with their corresponding letters. Hints are given to help you.

A	B	C	D	E	F	G	H	I	J
1	2	3	4	5	6	7	8	9	10
K	L	M	N	O	P	Q	R	S	T
11	12	13	14	15	16	17	18	19	20
U	V	W	X	Y	Z				
21	22	23	24	25	26				

A) **Hint:** A common nursery rhyme.
20 8 5   23 8 5 5 12 19   15 14   20 8 5   2 21 19   7 15 18   15 21 14 4   1 14 4   18 15 21 14 4

B) **Hint:** Four famous Greek gods.
26 5 21 19,   16 15 19 5 9 4 15 14,   8 1 4 5 19,   1 18 5 19

C) **Hint:** 'Take it Easy' words
4 1 23 4 12 5,   12 15 21 14 7 5,   4 1 12 12 25,   12 1 26 5,   18 5 19 20

D) **Hint:** Royal titles
17 21 5 5 14,   4 21 11 5,   5 13 16 5 18 15 18,   16 18 9 14 3 5 19 19,   2 1 18 15 14

E) **Hint:** How's the weather today?
3 15 12 4,   6 18 15 19 20 25,   9 3 25,   19 14 15 23 9 14 7, 6 18 15 26 5 14

Time taken: _____

PUZZLE 46: COUNTING CUBES   TIME LIMIT: 5 MINUTES

Count the cubes in the image below. Keep in mind that this image is in 3D and there may be some cubes that you cannot see.

Hint: Don't forget to count the cubes that are hidden behind or beneath the cubes that you can see.

A)

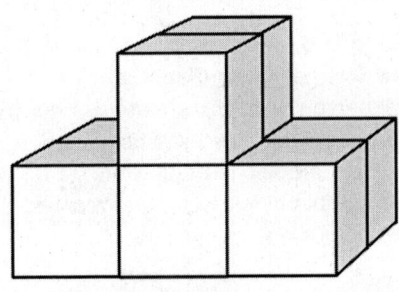

B)

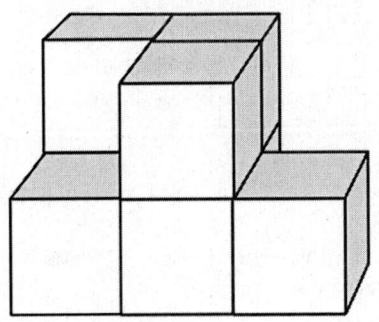

Time taken: _____

Bonus Puzzle: Letter Mash

C	J	F	A
K	D	L	I
N	E	B	M
G	P	O	H

Which letter is two places below the letter that is two to the right of the letter that is two above the letter that is immediately to the right of the letter that is four below the letter C?

Hint: Start from the end of the question and work backwards.

PUZZLE 47: CROSSWORD FAIRY TALE

Given below are clues that relate to fairy tales. Solve the clues to complete the crossword puzzle on the next page.

ACROSS
1. This lazy insect wasted the whole summer while the ants gathered food for the winter.
4. These three ___ ___ ___ ___ ___ ___ ___ ___ ___ ___ Gruff tried to cross a bridge that had a troll under it.
8. This princess lost her glass slipper at a ball.
10. This magical person gave (clue) 8 Across her glass slippers and told her she had to be back by midnight.
14. This princess ate a poisoned apple.
17. Jack climbed up this magic plant that reached the clouds.
18. Sister of (clue) 9 Down.

DOWN
2. This pauper found a magic lamp.
3. ___ ___ ___ ___ in Boots.
4. Ali ___ ___ ___ ___ and the 40 Thieves.
5. This naughty little girl ate up all the porridge and fell asleep in the house of the Three Bears.
6. The Princess and the ___ ___ ___.
7. This is the colour of the hood that a girl wore to visit her grandmother.
9. This brother and his sister (9 Across) found a gingerbread house in the middle of the woods.
11. This princess was locked in a tower and had long hair that she could let down over the window for people to climb up.
12. This person played his magic pipe and led all the children out of Hamelin.
13. 'Run, run as fast as you can! You can't catch me; I'm the ___ ___ ___ ___ ___ ___bread man!'
15. This Little Red ___ ___ ___ found some wheat and made bread with it, despite all the other farm animals refusing to help her.
16. This over confident ___ ___ ___ ___ decided to take a nap and lost the race to a tortoise!

TIME LIMIT: 20 MINUTES

Time taken: _____

Riddle Me This

I have a tongue but cannot talk,
I go for regular walks,
Yet I don't have legs,
No, not even a peg.
What am I?

PUZZLE 48: HASHI

Connect all islands with bridges.

Rules
1. The number of bridges coming in and going out from each island needs to be the same as the number inside the island.
2. You can only draw horizontal and vertical lines to connect islands. No diagonal lines are allowed.
3. Bridges cannot cut across each other or any of the islands.
4. You can draw one line to represent one bridge.
5. There cannot be more than two bridges for each pair of islands (although there can be more bridges leading away from the island to a different island). The total number of bridges per island can be anywhere from one to eight, depending on the number inside the island.
6. All islands must be connected so that if you start at one island, you should be able to travel to every other island using the bridges.

Hint
Start with an island where you know for sure which direction the bridges go. For example, in the image below, there cannot be any horizontal bridges for the number 2 in the third column from the left. Therefore, you know for sure that both bridges will have to connect to the number 7 below. Look at the example given below.

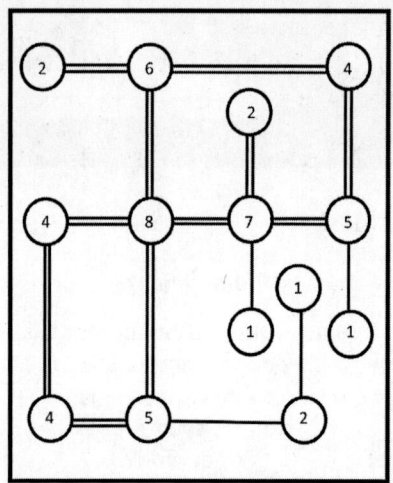

TIME LIMIT: 20 MINUTES

A) **Hint:** Start with Island 6 in the third row.

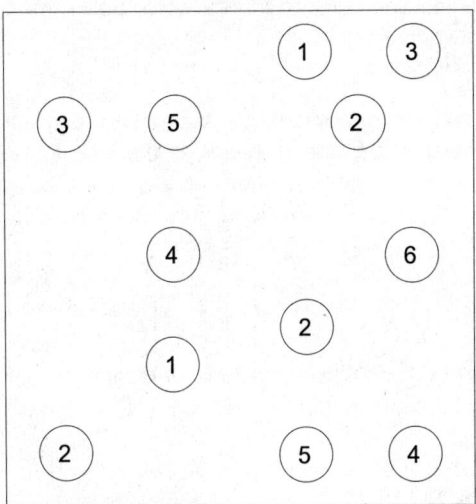

B) **Hint:** Start with Island 6 in the first row.

Time taken: _____

PUZZLE 49: LETTER SLIDES   TIME LIMIT: 10 MINUTES

Letter slides are formed by starting at one letter and sliding your way to a connecting letter to form a word. Solve the clues below to find words.

Rules
1. Words can be formed only by sliding from one letter to another letter that is either above, below, to the left, right or diagonal to the previous letter. You cannot skip letters to reach another letter.
2. You cannot use the same letter more than once in any word.

O	P	I	A
H	S	T	L

Clues
A) To move by jumping on one foot. (3 letters)
B) When you want to buy something, you go to a __ __ __ __ (4 letters)
C) A type of bread. (4 letters)
D) You go to a __ __ __ __ office to send letters to people. (4 letters)
E) A hole. (3 letters)
F) The food tasted so bad that I had to __ __ __ __ it out. (4 letters)
G) You kiss somebody by using these. (4 letters)
H) The opposite of 'stand.' (3 letters)
I) The puppy was wagging its __ __ __ __. (4 letters)
J) Can you guess what the 8-letter word is? (**Hint:** It's a place that you go to, for getting treatment when you are sick.)

Time taken: _____

Bonus Game: Opposites Attract

Jumbled letters for two words that are opposites of each other are given below. Figure out the words and fill them into the grid.

FNDIR   NMYE

PUZZLE 50: MATH WHIZ   TIME LIMIT: 10 MINUTES

Solve the following mathematical links to get your final answer. Try to solve them in your head without writing anything down or using a calculator. Just follow the links downwards and solve the mathematical instructions given in each link. Once you have the answer, move to the next link below.

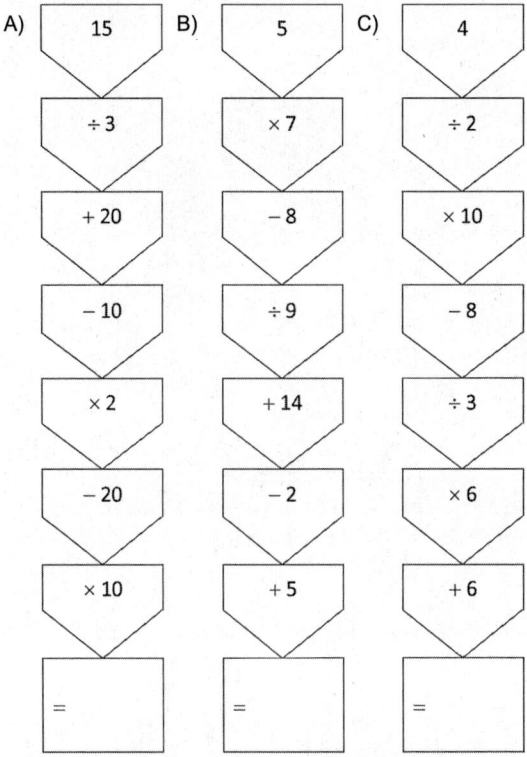

Time taken: _____

What Comes Next?

Look at the sequence of numbers below and try to figure out what number should replace the question mark.

1, 4, 7, 10, 13, 16, ?

MEDIUM PUZZLES

PUZZLE 51: MAZE AMAZE TIME LIMIT: 10 MINUTES

Time taken: _____

PUZZLE 52: WORD LADDERS

A word ladder is a sequence of words formed by just changing one letter at a time.

Rules
1. The first and last words are given. Working your way up or down the ladder, change only **one** letter in each word to get the next word—eventually ending with the final word.
2. All words have to be real words and not made-up words.
3. All words need to have the same number of letters as the first and last words. You cannot make the words longer or shorter.
4. The number of rungs in the ladder indicates how many words are needed to make the final word. In both examples 1 and 2, there are three words that are needed to make LESS to MORE and RATS to MICE respectively.

Look at the examples given below to get an idea of how to solve this puzzle.

Example 1: Change LESS to MORE

L	E	S	S
L	O	S	S
L	O	S	E
L	O	R	E
M	O	R	E

Example 2: Change RATS to MICE

R	A	T	S
M	A	T	S
M	A	T	E
M	I	T	E
M	I	C	E

TIME LIMIT: 10 MINUTES

A) Sign your NAME up to join the ARMY. Some clues are given to help you.

N	A	M	E
A	R	M	Y

A title given to a woman who is knighted by the queen.

These are built across rivers to stop the flow of water.

Becomes less bright.

What you need to do to shoot a target accurately (plural).

The upper part of your hands below your shoulders.

B) Abracadabra! Make this LION into a TOAD!

L	I	O	N
T	O	A	D

A silly or foolish person (slang).

Stolen treasure (slang).

A hooligan, thug or oaf.

Noisy.

Something heavy that you carry is called a ___ ___ ___ ___.

Time taken: _____

Bonus Game: Assembling a Word Square

Arrange the tiles to form a 4x4 square such that the words read the same across and down. Look at Puzzles 14, 39, 64 and 89 to get an idea of what word squares are.

Tiles: `P / END`, `PE / E`, `FR / R`, `O / OP / M`, `OM`

PUZZLE 53: DOMINO TWIST

Places the dominoes in their correct places.

Rules
1. Place the eight dominoes in the spaces provided.
2. Each domino piece can be rotated to fit into the space.
3. The domino piece that you place must match the piece already provided. For example, if the edge piece has 5 dots on it, the domino that you place next to it also needs to have 5 dots.

Hints
1. If you have domino pieces at home, you can use those to help you solve this puzzle.
2. You can trace out the eight domino pieces on a different piece of paper, cut them out and then place them on the puzzle. This makes it easier to rotate the pieces to see where they may fit.
3. Start with the domino that you know will definitely fit into a specific place.

Look at the example below to see how to match the dominoes.

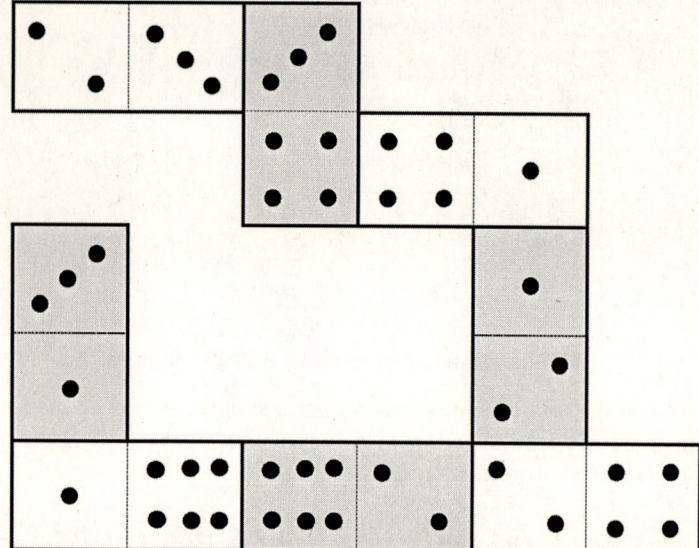

TIME LIMIT: 10 MINUTES

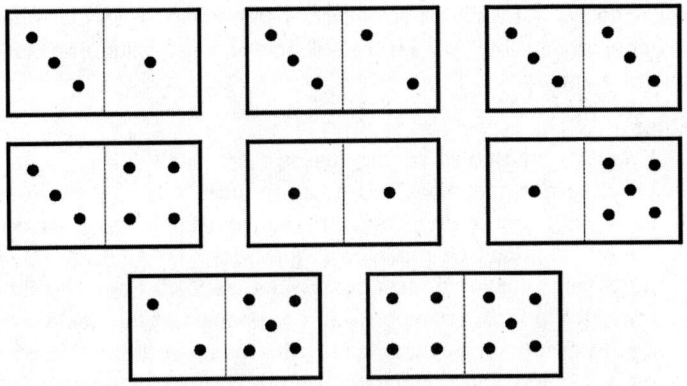

Place the dominoes above in the figure below.

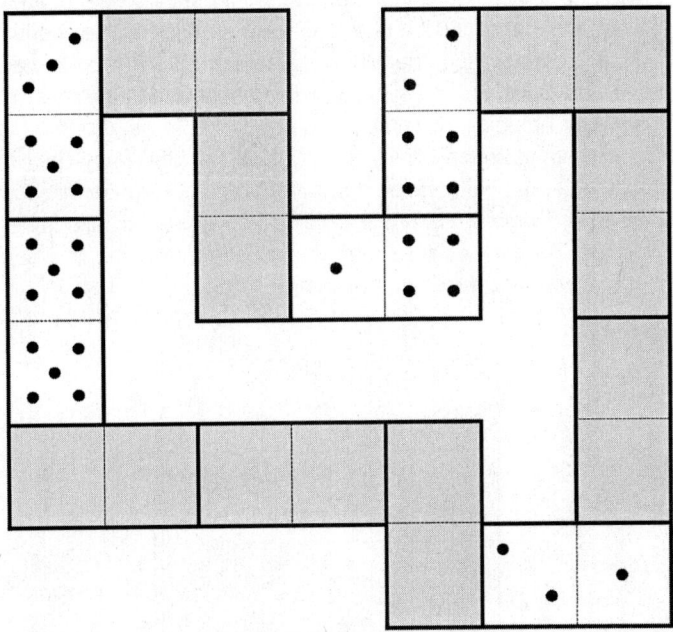

Time taken: _____

PUZZLE 54: MINI SUDOKU

TIME LIMIT: 10 MINUTES

Given below is a mini Sudoku puzzle that involves an 8x8 grid of squares divided into 4x2 blocks. Fill in the blank squares with the correct numbers.

Rules
1. Every square should contain just one number.
2. Only the numbers from 1 to 8 can be used.
3. Each 4x2 block must contain all numbers from 1 to 8. None of the numbers can be repeated in the block.
4. Each vertical column must contain the numbers from 1 to 8 only once. None of the numbers can be repeated in the column.
5. Each horizontal row must contain the numbers from 1 to 8 only once. None of the numbers can be repeated in the rows.

Hints
1. When you start the Sudoku puzzle, some squares will already be filled with numbers. Use those numbers as clues for blank squares.
2. Start by identifying the blank squares that give you a definite answer. Once you do this, you will be able to deduce other blank squares around that number.
3. Some blank squares may initially look like they may hold more than one possible number. Pencil in all possible numbers and move on to the next blank square. Once you figure out a number for certain, go back to the squares that have more than one answer and erase that number from that square.

Example:

5	3	2	7	1	8	4	6
1	4	6	8	7	3	2	5
8	5	3	6	2	1	7	4
2	7	4	1	3	6	5	8
3	1	8	5	4	7	6	2
6	2	7	4	8	5	3	1
7	8	5	2	6	4	1	3
4	6	1	3	5	2	8	7

TIME LIMIT: 10 MINUTES

A)

2	1				5	4	
		7	4	2			1
	3	1				5	2
			5	7	6		
5		2		6	1		
7		8			3		4
4	8				7	3	
1			6			8	5

B)

	2	3				4	
	5	6	4	1	7		
	8	1		5		7	6
	7		3		2	8	
2			6	3	5		7
5		7		2	4		
	6	4	8	7		5	
7	1	2		8			4

Time taken: _____

PUZZLE 55: COIN BOARD

TIME LIMIT: 10 MINUTES

Look at the 6x6 grid on the next page. Place two coins on each row, so that each row, column and two main diagonals contain only two coins.

Rules
1. You can place only one coin on a square.
2. Each row, column and main diagonal must contain only two coins.

Hints
1. You can use real coins for this puzzle or simply shade in the squares on which you would place a coin. You need 12 coins.
2. Start at the centre and work your way outwards.

Look at the example given below to get an idea of the completed puzzle.

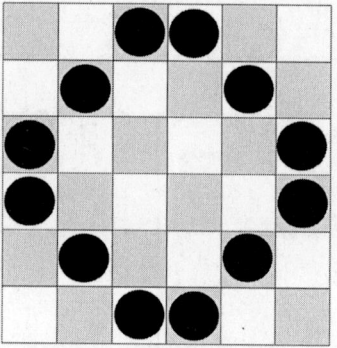

Bonus Game: Tic-Tac-Toe

This is a game of Tic-Tac-Toe or noughts and crosses that has already been started. The aim is to get either three noughts (O) or three crosses (X) in a row. In this game, player X has already played three times and it is your move now. Where would you place the **O** so that you win no matter where the other player places the next **X**?

O		X
		X
O	X	O

TIME LIMIT: 10 MINUTES

Solve the puzzles below. Four coins are already placed to help you get started.

A)

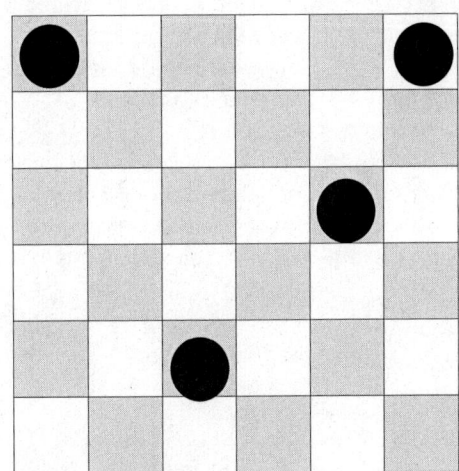

B)

Time taken: _____

PUZZLE 56: WORD SWIRL   TIME LIMIT: 10 MINUTES

How many words of four or more letters can you make from the following word swirl?

Rules
1. Follow the clues below to find the word.
2. Each word must have the centre letter (P) in it.
3. All words have to be real words and not made up.

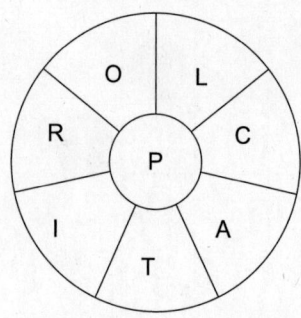

Clues
1. This person can fly an aeroplane. (5 letters)
2. This white bear lives in the Arctic, on ice-covered waters. (5 letters)
3. A general subject of conversation. (5 letters)
4. A ___ ___ ___ ___ (area) of land. (4 letters)
5. A slang word for a policeman. (3 letters)
6. A set of two things is called a ___ ___ ___ ___. (4 letters)
7. A small hole. (3 letters)
8. A doorway to a different dimension. (6 letters)
9. Another word for the front porch of your house. (5 letters)
10. When you make a deal with somebody, it is called a ___ ___ ___ ___. (4 letters)

Bonus: Can you guess the 8-letter word?

Time taken: _____

Fun Fact
Recent studies show that solving puzzles and practicing a second language every day can improve your thinking, memory and concentration!

PUZZLE 57: FOLDING CUBES TIME LIMIT: 10 MINUTES

How many of the following cube nets can form three-dimensional cubes when they are folded?

Rules
1. Imagine that each shape is folded along its lines. You will have to manipulate the shapes in your mind and see which cube nets form cubes. If you find it hard to do this, trace or draw the shapes on a separate piece of paper and physically fold them on their lines to see if it makes a cube.
2. There should not be any overlapping flaps.

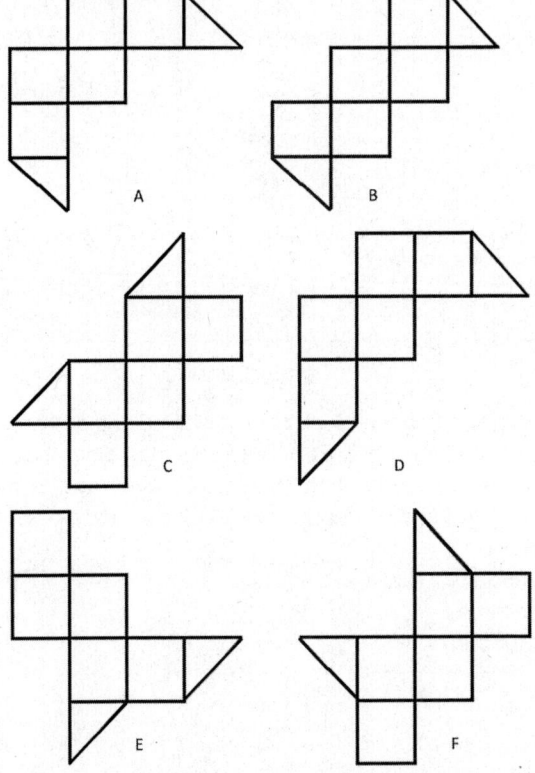

Time taken: _____

PUZZLE 58: WORD SEARCH– C

Find and circle the following words in the word search puzzle on the next page. All words begin with the letter C. The words can be found horizontally, vertically or diagonally, in any direction (back to front or bottom to top). There are 30 words to find in 30 minutes so try and find all the words as quickly as possible!

- Cabbage
- Cabinet
- Cocoon
- Captive
- Calcium
- Callers
- Calmest
- Calorie
- Calming
- Camera
- Candle
- Canyon
- Crayon
- Captain
- Capsule
- Captive
- Charcoal
- Cutting
- Cycling
- Cyclone
- Crystal
- Cuckoo
- Coupon
- Crowbar
- Crowded
- Camphor
- Caramel
- Chats
- Caravan
- Catfish

Bonus Puzzle

Four friends were sharing a pizza. They decided that the oldest friend would get the extra piece. Suzy is two months older than Jane, who is three months younger than Jemima. Elizabeth is one month older than Jane. Who should get the extra piece of pizza?
a) Suzy
b) Jane
c) Jemima
d) Elizabeth

TIME LIMIT: 30 MINUTES

Time taken: _____

PUZZLE 59: SLITHERLINKS

TIME LIMIT: 20 MINUTES

The objective of this puzzle is to use the numbers inside the squares as guides to help you draw horizontal or vertical 'fences' around the entire puzzle to form a simple loop, with no open ends. The numbers 1, 2 and 3 inside the squares represent the number of fences or loops around that particular number. This puzzle requires pure logic to solve and does not involve any guess work.

Rules
1. The fence or loop has to be a single continuous line throughout the puzzle. All line segments must be connected.
2. The loop cannot touch or cross itself at any point. It also cannot be left open at any point.
3. The number of fences around a particular number should correspond to that number. For example, if the number is 2, then only two fences can be drawn around that number, either to the left, right, top or bottom of the number.
4. If there is no number in a square, you can draw any number of lines surrounding that square in order to connect the loop to numbered squares.

Hints
1. If the number of fences surrounding a square correspond to the number in the square, all other possible horizontal and vertical lines surrounding that square can be eliminated.
2. Start with a number which points to a definite fence. For example, if there is a 3 in the corner, you know for sure that the two outside edges need to be drawn. That leaves only the two inside edges, which can be deduced using the other numbers surrounding it.

Example:

3			0	1	0	
	3	3	3	3	2	
2		0		0	3	
1		3		2		0
	0					2
3	3		2	0	1	
		2				3

TIME LIMIT: 20 MINUTES

A)

2	3	3	3	3	3	2
3					0	3
		3				
	2				2	
2	3	2		3		
				1		3
3			2	1	2	2

B)

		3			3		
3	2		1	1	1		
		3					3
2	2	2		2		3	
2			2				
2				1	1	1	3
2		3					
3			2	3	2	1	

Time taken: _____

Bonus: Rebus Puzzle

A Rebus puzzle is a picture representation of a common word, saying or phrase. For example, /R/E/A/D/I/N/G/ could be interpreted as 'Reading between the lines'. Try and solve the following Rebus puzzles.

1.	2.	3.	4.
O N C E TIME	◆ ○	IMPORTANT = IMPORTANT	ELEPHANT

PUZZLE 60: JOBS AND CAREERS REVERSE CROSSWORD

TIME LIMIT: 10 MINUTES

Place each answer in its correct slot. This puzzle requires pure logic to solve and does not involve any guess work. Fit all the mythical creatures into their correct boxes.

12-Letter Words
Veterinarian
Receptionist
Web developer
Event planner

10-Letter Words
Accountant
Architects

7-letter words
Captain
Dentist
Painter
Analyst

6-Letter Words
Doctor
Police
Artist

5-letter words
Pilot
Clerk

Time taken: _____

PUZZLE 61: WORD PYRAMID

TIME LIMIT: 10 MINUTES

Beginning at the top, add a letter to a box at each step, moving towards the bottom seven-letter word. Solve each clue and write the answer in each corresponding row.

Rules
1. The same letter or letters should be used in the next row plus an additional letter.
2. The letters may be rearranged to form a new word.
3. Each word should correspond to the given clue.

Follow the clues to fill in the word pyramid.

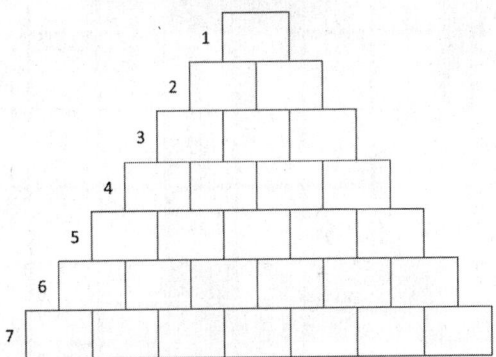

Clues
1. Thirteenth letter of the alphabet.
2. A mantra chanted at the beginning and end of yoga sessions. Also said to be the sound that vibrates across the universe.
3. The sound that cows make.
4. Uncultivated land usually covered with heather.
5. Something that you use to sweep the floor.
6. Somebody born during a baby boom can also be called a ___ ___ ___ ___ ___ ___ (informal).
7. Room where you sleep.

Bonus Game
Rearrange letters in the last word, can you find two more 7-letter words?

Time taken: _____

PUZZLE 62: LOOPY LOOPS

Draw a single loop that passes through the centre of every white square, using only horizontal and vertical lines. The loop cannot pass through any square more than once, cannot cross itself or pass through any of the black squares.

Look at the example given below to get an idea of the completed puzzle.

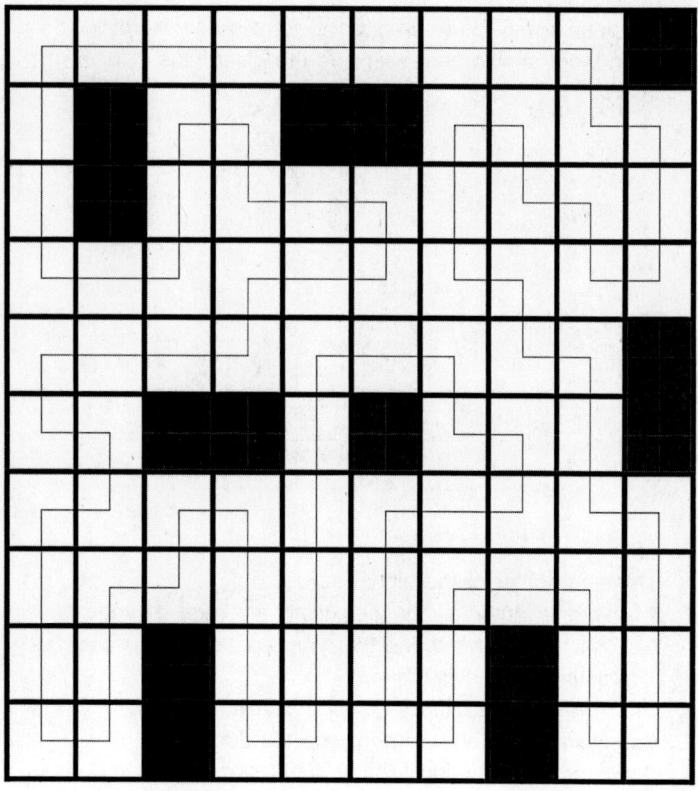

TIME LIMIT: 20 MINUTES

Time taken: _____

Bonus Game: Missing Vowels

Fill in the missing vowels in the following words.

1. FTR
2. CVL
3. SCHL
4. DTD
5. DRM

PUZZLE 63: WHAT COMES NEXT?

Look at the sequences of tiles below and logically work out what answer should fit into the blank box at the end. Try to work out the plan, scheme or order behind every row and column of tiles. Choose your answer from options A to E. Each question may require a different kind of logic to solve it.

Looking at the example below, going row-wise, we can see that with each consecutive tile, the black squares rotate clockwise by one square. Therefore, Option A would fit into the empty space.

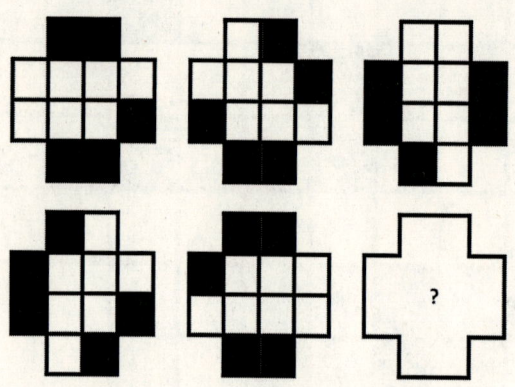

Options:

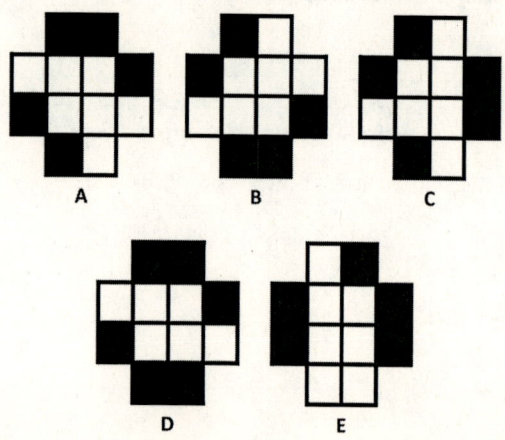

TIME LIMIT: 10 MINUTES

Find the missing tile from Options A to E.

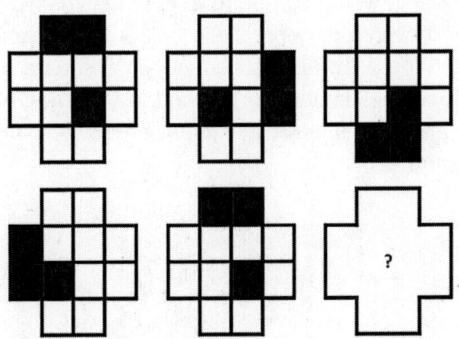

Options:

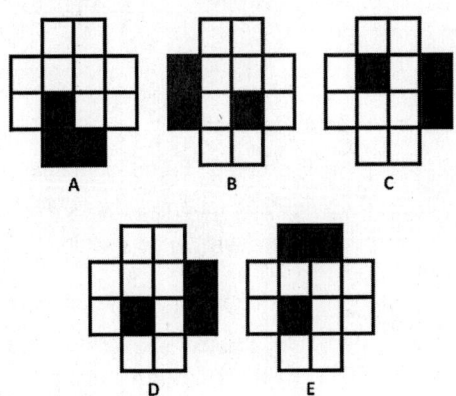

Time taken: _____

Bonus Game: Find the Odd One Out

Find the odd word out of all the following words:
1. Crab, Tortoise, Fish, Frog
2. Piano, Guitar, Cello, Harp
3. Slippers, Socks, Gloves, Shoes
4. 10, 14, 20, 25, 28, 30
5. Apple, Banana, Cabbage, Mango

PUZZLE 64: WORD SQUARES TIME LIMIT: 10 MINUTES

Word squares consist of a set of words written in a grid in such a way that the same words can be read both horizontally and vertically. The number of words is generally equal to the number of letters in each word. All the words cross perfectly in a square arrangement.

You are given clues that correspond to the rows. All you need to do is write down the answer horizontally and vertically to complete the word square.

Example:

B	O	S	S
O	R	E	O
S	E	L	F
S	O	F	A

A person who is in charge of a person, group or organization.

The brand name of a chocolate biscuit with a cream filling.

Me, My___ ___ ___ ___ and I.

A couch.

Work out the word squares below:

A)

Attempt to do something. E.g. I took a___ ___ ___ ___ (try) at it.

Present tense of had.

An appliance in which cakes are baked.

A portable shelter that you can sleep in when you go camping.

B)

The place where you live.

It was once locked, now it is ___ ___ ___ ___.

To repair.

Finishes.

Time taken: _____

PUZZLE 65: WORD CIRCLES

TIME LIMIT: 10 MINUTES

Given below are eight-letter words arranged in circles. They are not jumbled. Find the correct word and write it down. The words can be read clockwise or counterclockwise.

1.   A C
    T   C
    N   I
        E D

Answer: _____

2.   D N
    I   O
    V   I
        I S

Answer: _____

3.   R O
    M   F
    P   T
        L A

Answer: _____

4.   S H
    T   T
    R   G
        E N

Answer: _____

5.   A L
    U   L
    M   E
        B R

Answer: _____

6.   I D
    S   E
    C   S
        L O

Answer: _____

7.   T A
    I   L
    P   H
        S O

Answer: _____

8.   N G
    I   S
    N   T
        N U

Answer: _____

9.   D L
    L   I
    I   F
        W E

Answer: _____

10.   O M
    R   O
    R   T
        O W

Answer: _____

Time taken: _____

PUZZLE 66: REVERSE MINESWEEPER

Reverse minesweeper is a puzzle that begins with all the answers revealed. You will need to place mines around the number squares. The number of mines around a number square corresponds to the number of the square. For example, if the number is 2, it indicates that there are two mines in the immediate squares that surround it.

Rules
1. Place a mine into the empty squares that surround each number, including diagonally adjacent squares. You can either draw a mine or shade the cell to represent the mine.
2. The number of mines around a number needs to correspond to the value of the number.

Hints
1. There may be blank squares as well. Mark these off with an X so that you don't get confused.
2. Start with a square that you know for sure is a mine.

Look at the example given below to get an idea of the completed puzzle.

●	2					1	2	●
2	●		1	1	2	●	3	
1		1		●	2			●
			3	●	3		3	3
			2	●			●	●
								2
	●	1	1	1		●	1	
			2	●	2	1	2	
		●	2					●

TIME LIMIT: 10 MINUTES

Place 20 mines in the puzzle below. (**Hint:** Block off all the squares around the 0 squares first to eliminate them.)

	2		0		0			3
2								
	2			0			2	2
0			2			2		0
		0						
		2	4		8		3	0
								1
	3			3	4		2	
	2		0				1	

Time taken: _____

Bonus Game: Code Decode

The following are pairs of letters that hide a word. Strike one letter from each pair to reveal the word. For example: HS AG MR AP. The word revealed is HARP.

1. BH AE BM DY
2. SC MO IO LB
3. FE BA CM BT
4. GO KA NM EV
5. JQ UO IC PN

PUZZLE 67: MATCHING SHAPES   TIME LIMIT: 10 MINUTES

Draw lines to match each identical shape. The lines must not cross each other or touch each other. There must never be more than one connecting line in any square. All lines have to be horizontal or vertical lines only. No diagonal lines are allowed. Look at the example given below to get an idea of the completed puzzle.

Connect the identical shapes in the following puzzle.

Time taken: _____

PUZZLE 68: TANGRAM
TIME LIMIT: 10 MINUTES

Using all seven tangram shapes from the beginning of the book, make the figure of the boat below. You can cut out the shapes from the book, trace the shapes on a different sheet of paper and cut them out, or use Tangram blocks, if you have them.

Rules
1. All seven pieces must be used.
2. All seven pieces must touch each other.
3. None of the pieces should overlap.

Time taken: _____

Bonus Game: Anagrams

An anagram is a word that can be formed by rearranging the letters of another word. For example, LOOPED is an anagram of POODLE. Find the anagram for the words that are the capital letters.
1. He used the BRUSH to draw a ___ ___ ___ ___ ___.
2. When the SALES begin, we can buy the stuffed ___ ___ ___ ___ ___.
3. She wrote in her DIARY about her allergy to ___ ___ ___ ___ ___.
4. She had a ROOM overlooking the ___ ___ ___ ___.
5. Out WEST, we get the best chicken ___ ___ ___ ___.

PUZZLE 69: DIVIDING SHAPES

Divide the following figure into equal parts by drawing along the lines of the inner squares.

Rules
1. Each of the divided shapes should be identical to each other.
2. There should be no added or left out squares.
3. If all divided parts are rotated to face the same direction, they should all be exactly the same size and should look exactly alike.

Hint
Count the squares inside the figure and divide the total by the total required. This will give you an idea of how many squares are needed inside the figure.

In the following example, the figure needs to be divided by **four** equal parts.

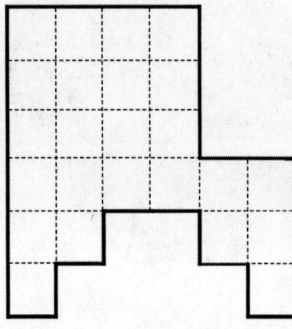

Answer:

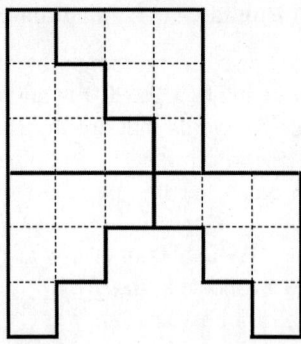

TIME LIMIT: 10 MINUTES

A. Divide this shape into four equal parts.

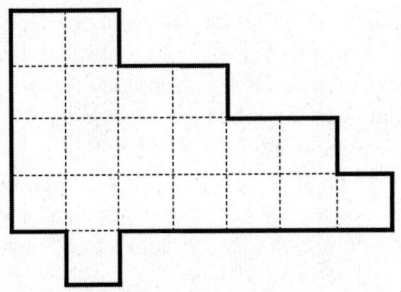

B. Divide this shape into five equal parts.

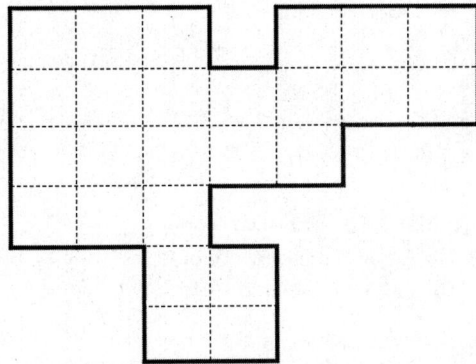

Time taken: _____

Bonus Game: Connect Loops

Connect all the lines to form a single loop. The line has to touch all 4 corners of every square and must not touch or cross any other lines.

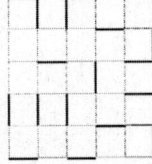

PUZZLE 70: CODE DECODE

TIME LIMIT: 20 MINUTES

Do you remember the Caesar Cipher from exercise 20 and the Polybius Cipher from exercise 45? The following puzzle is a combination of the two ciphers. As mentioned in Puzzle 20, Caesar's magic number was 3, which means that each letter was shifted by 3 places on the alphabet either to the right or to the left of the given letter. The Polybius Cipher is just substituting corresponding letters to the numbers in the code. Hints and clues are given to help you. Don't forget that while the Caesar Cipher moves 3 spaces either to the left or right, the Polybius Cipher just substitutes letters and does not move to other letters.

A	B	C	D	E	F	G	H	I	J	K	L	M
1	2	3	4	5	6	7	8	9	10	11	12	13
N	O	P	Q	R	S	T	U	V	W	X	Y	Z
14	15	16	17	18	19	20	21	22	23	24	25	26

A) I live in a …
F D E L 14,   22 L O 12 D,   1 S 1 18 W 13 H 14 W,   8 X W

Clues:
1. There are 3 Ts in the last two words.
2. There are 2 As in the first two words.
3. There are 2 Ls in the second word.

B) Hobbies
J D U 4 5 Q L 14 J,   I L 19 K L 14 J,   3 U R 3 K H 20,   1 18 W

Clues:
1. There are 2 Gs in the first word.
2. There are 2 Is in the second word.
3. There are 2 Cs in the third word.

C) How I talk
D F F H Q 20,   S 9 W F 8,   W R 14 H,   4 L F W L 15 14

Clues:
1. There are 2 Cs in the first word.
2. The second word starts with the letter P.
3. There are 2 Is in the last word.

Time taken: _____

PUZZLE 71: COUNTING CUBES   TIME LIMIT: 5 MINUTES

Count the cubes in the images below. Keep in mind that the images are in 3D and there may be some cubes that you cannot see.

Hint: Don't forget to count the cubes that are hidden behind or beneath the cubes that you can see.

A)

B)

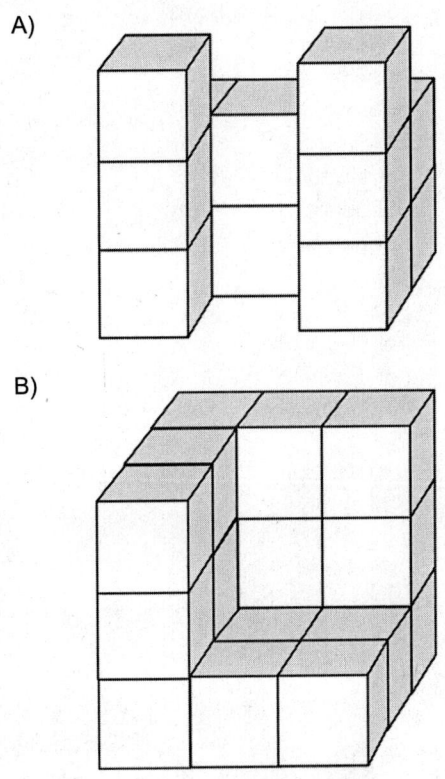

Time taken: _____

Riddle Me This

Stare at me and you may go blind,
Yet, you cannot see if I don't shine.
What am I?

PUZZLE 72: CROSSWORD GROUPS   TIME LIMIT: 20 MINUTES

Collective nouns are names for a group or collection of people or things. Examples: a flock of birds, a pack of wolves, a herd of cows, etc. Given below are clues that relate to groups of animals, people or things. Solve the clues to complete the crossword puzzle.

Across
3. A _____ of seagulls.
5. A _____ of names.
7. A _____ of fish.
9. A _____ of rain.
11. A _____ of salmon.
12. A _____ of actors.
14. A _____ of pearls.
17. A _____ of arrows.
19. An _____ of ants.
21. A _____ of film.
22. A _____ of cotton.
23. A _____ of colours.

Down
1. A _____ of cars.
2. An _____ of maps.
4. A _____ of singers.
6. A _____ of hares.
8. A _____ of drawers.
10. A _____ of bees.
13. A _____ of natives.
15. A _____ of light.
16. A _____ of geese.
18. A _____ of mountains.
20. A _____ of rioters.

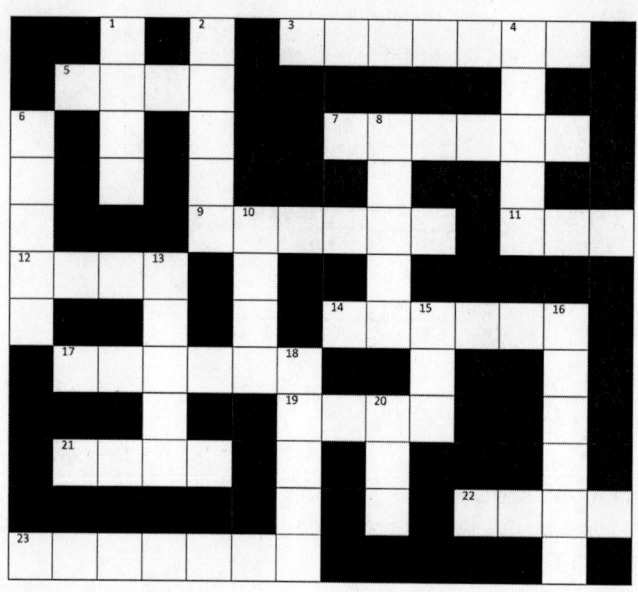

PUZZLE 73: HASHI TIME LIMIT: 20 MINUTES

Connect all islands with bridges.

Rules
1. The number of bridges coming in and going out from each island needs to be the same as the number inside the island.
2. You can only draw horizontal and vertical lines to connect islands. No diagonal lines are allowed.
3. Bridges cannot cut across each other or any of the islands.
4. You can draw one line to represent one bridge.
5. There cannot be more than two bridges for each pair of islands (although there can be more bridges leading away from the island to a different island). The total number of bridges per island can be anywhere from one to eight, depending on the number inside the island.
6. All islands must be connected so that if you start at one island, you should be able to travel to every other island using the bridges.

Hint
Start with an island where you know for sure which direction the bridges go. For example, in the image below, there cannot be any horizontal bridges for the number 2 on the left column. Therefore, you know for sure that both bridges will have to connect to the number 5 above it. Look at the example given below to get an idea of the completed puzzle.

(Clue: Start with island 6 on the second row.)

Time taken: _____

PUZZLE 74: LETTER SLIDES

TIME LIMIT: 10 MINUTES

Letter Slides are formed by starting at one letter and sliding your way to a connecting letter to form a word. Solve the clues below to find words.

Rules
1. Words can be formed only by sliding from one letter to another that is either above, below, to the left, right or diagonal to the previous letter. You cannot skip letters to reach another letter.
2. You cannot use the same letter more than once in any word.

R	R	E	T	S
Y	B	W	A	R

Clues
A) A small, hard boil or growth on the skin. (4 letters)
B) A thin, hollow tube that you can suck your juice through. (5 letters)
C) 'Twinkle, twinkle, little __ __ __ __.' (4 letters)
D) The liquid or fluid that forms the seas, lakes and rivers. (5 letters)
E) This furry mammal with a short tail lives in the Arctic on ice-covered waters. (4 letters)
F) 'Although she was a widow, she did not __ __ __ __ black to the funeral.' (4 letters)
G) 'This city has the lowest crime __ __ __ __ in the world!' (4 letters)
H) 'His tears made his cheeks __ __ __.' (3 letters)
I) A word that completes the names of these fruits: blue, black, rasp and cran. (5 letters)
J) Can you guess what the 10-letter word is? (**Hint:** It's a word that combines the answers to questions B and I.)

Time taken: _____

Bonus Game: Number Slides

Fill in the grid below with numbers from 1–16 such that each number is either above, below, to the left or right of the previous number and next number. You cannot move diagonally.

1		3	
12		10	
	16		
			7

PUZZLE 75: MATH WHIZ   TIME LIMIT: 10 MINUTES

Solve the following mathematical links to get your final answer. Try to solve them in your head without writing anything down or using a calculator. Just follow the links downwards and solve the mathematical instructions given in each link. Once you have the answer, move to the next link below.

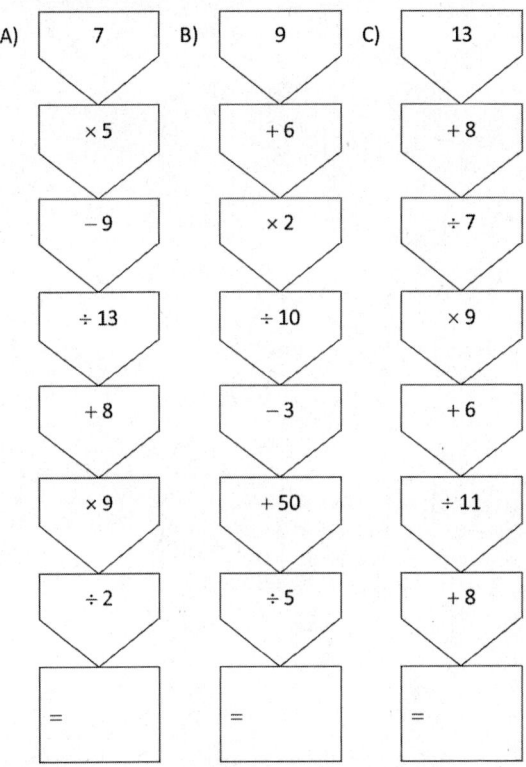

Time taken: _____

What Comes Next?

Look at the sequence of numbers below and try to figure out what number should replace the question mark.

5, 15, 25, 35, 45, ?

DIFFICULT PUZZLES

PUZZLE 76: MAZE AMAZE   TIME LIMIT: 10 MINUTES

Find your way out of this tricky maze. Start at the entrance and work your way to the exit.

Time taken: _____

PUZZLE 77: WORD LADDERS

A word ladder is a sequence of words formed by just changing one letter at a time.

Rules
1. The first and last words are given. Working your way up or down the ladder, change only **one** letter in each word to get the next word—ending with the final word.
2. All words have to be real words and not made-up words.
3. All words need to have the same number of letters as the first and last words. You cannot make the words longer or shorter.
4. The number of rungs in the ladder inidicates how many words are needed to make the final word. In example 1, there are three words that are needed to make GOLD into BELL and in example 2, there are five rungs that are needed to make SCAR into WAND.

Look at the examples given below to get an idea of how to solve this puzzle.

Example 1: Change GOLD to BELL

G	O	L	D
B	O	L	D
B	A	L	D
B	A	L	L
B	E	L	L

Example 2: Change SCAR to WAND

S	C	A	R
S	E	A	R
S	E	E	R
S	E	E	D
S	E	N	D
S	A	N	D
W	A	N	D

TIME LIMIT: 10 MINUTES

A) Change HEAD to TAIL. Some clues are given to help you.

H	E	A	D
T	A	I	L

A doctor can help ___ ___ ___ ___ a sick person.

A dark greenish-blue colour.

'Can you ___ ___ ___ ___ her to go away?'

Opposite of short.

B) SLOW DOWN in four steps.

S	L	O	W
D	O	W	N

A slit or space in a machine for a coin to be inserted.

A black powder that you find in fire places or chimneys.

'How ___ ___ ___ ___ (quickly) can you come here?'

'This field used to be ___ ___ ___ ___ with wheat.'

Time taken: _____

Bonus Game: Assembling a Word Square

Arrange the tiles to form a 4x4 square such that the words read the same across and down. Look at Puzzles 14, 39, 64 and 89 to get an idea of what word squares are.

| L |
| E |

A	V
	A
	L

| P |
| L |
| O |

| | V |
| T | A |

| L | O | T |
| | | A |

PUZZLE 78: DOMINO TWIST

Place the dominoes in their correct places.

Rules
1. Place the eight dominoes in the spaces provided.
2. Each domino piece can be rotated to fit into the space.
3. The domino piece that you place must match the piece already provided. For example, if the edge piece has 5 dots on it, the domino that you place next to it also needs to have 5 dots.

Hints
1. If you have domino pieces at home, you can use those to help you solve this puzzle.
2. You can trace out the eight domino pieces on a sheet of paper, cut them out and then place them on the puzzle. This makes it easier to rotate the pieces to see where they may fit.
3. Start with the domino that you know will definitely fit into a specific place.

Look at the example below to see how to match the dominoes.

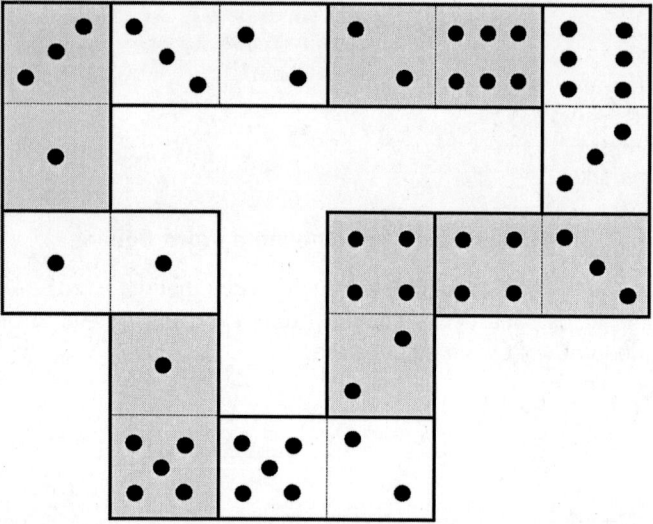

TIME LIMIT: 10 MINUTES

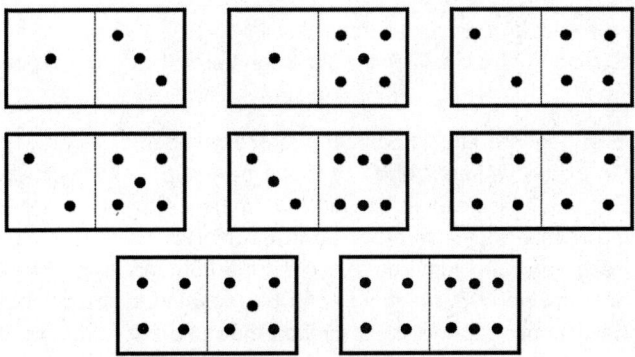

Place the dominoes above in the figure below.

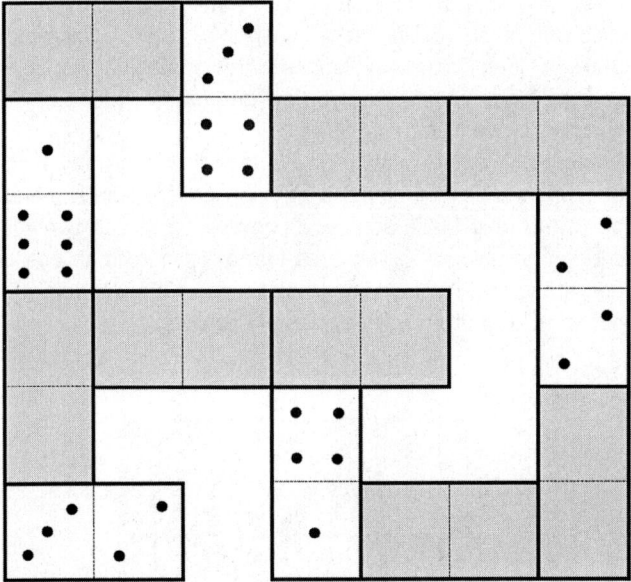

Time taken: _____

PUZZLE 79: SUDOKU

Given below is a Sudoku puzzle that involves a 9x9 grid of squares divided into 3x3 blocks. Fill in the blank squares with the correct numbers.

Rules
1. Every square should contain just one number.
2. Only the numbers from 1 to 9 can be used.
3. Each 3x3 block must contain all numbers from 1 to 9. None of the numbers can be repeated in the block.
4. Each vertical column must contain the numbers from 1 to 9 only once. None of the numbers can be repeated in the column.
5. Each horizontal row must contain the numbers from 1 to 9 only once. None of the numbers can be repeated in the rows.

Hints
1. When you start the Sudoku puzzle, some squares will already be filled with numbers. Use those numbers as clues for blank squares.
2. Start by identifying the blank squares that give you a definite answer. Once you do this, you will be able to deduce other blank squares around that number.
3. Some blank squares may initially look like they may hold more than one possible number. Pencil in all possible numbers and move on to the next blank square. Once you figure out a number for certain, go back to the squares that have more than one answer and erase that number from that square. This will help eliminate numbers until you arrive at just one answer.

Example:

1	5	3	2	6	7	4	9	8
9	4	7	1	8	5	2	6	3
6	2	8	9	3	4	5	7	1
3	1	2	6	7	8	9	5	4
5	6	9	4	2	3	1	8	7
7	8	4	5	9	1	6	3	2
2	3	5	7	1	9	8	4	6
4	7	6	8	5	2	3	1	9
8	9	1	3	4	6	7	2	5

TIME LIMIT: 10 MINUTES

7	6							3
	4	8	7	6		2	1	
	3		2				7	
6	1	3		4			5	9
			6	3	5	8		
8					9			
4		9			6		2	8
				8	4			
1	8		9			3	6	4

Time taken: _____

Bonus Game: Opposites Attract

Shuffled letters to two words that are opposites of each other are given below. Figure out the words and fill them into the grid.

PDOR HBMEL

PUZZLE 80: COIN BOARD

Look at the 8x8 grid on the next page. Place two coins on each row, so that each row, column and the two main diagonals contain only two coins.

Rules
1. You can place only one coin on a square.
2. Each row, column and main diagonal must contain only two coins.

Hints
1. You can use real coins for this puzzle or simply shade in the squares on which you would place a coin. You need 16 coins.
2. Start at the centre and work your way outwards.

Look at the example given below to get an idea of the completed puzzle.

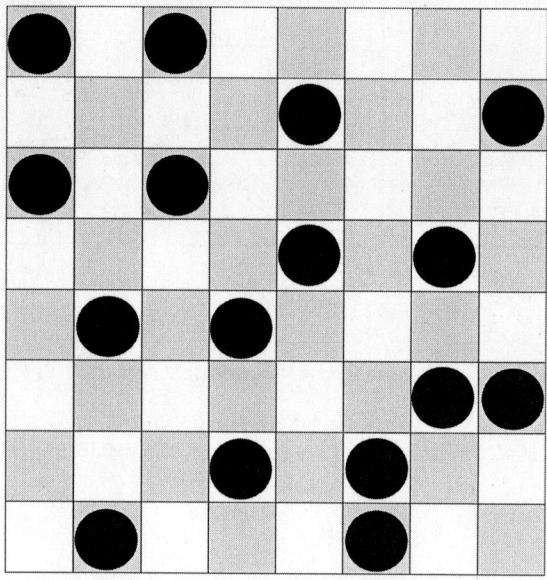

TIME LIMIT: 10 MINUTES

Solve the puzzle below. Five coins are already placed to help you get started.

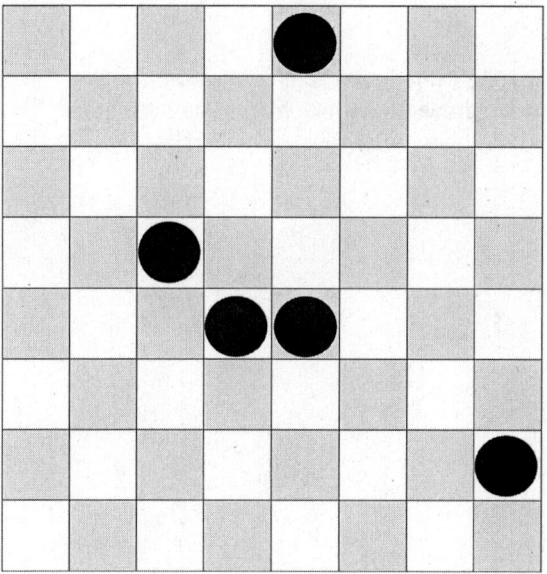

Time taken: _____

Whodunnit?

Luke was kidnapped and the kidnappers sent a ransom note to his family asking for a lot of money in unmarked notes. The money was to be put into a suitcase and kept under a bench in a nearby park. Luke's brother Thomas was to place the suitcase under the park bench that night at 8 p.m. sharp. However, while he was on his way to the bench, somebody hit him on his head from behind and ran away with the suitcase. When the police questioned him, Thomas said, 'It was very dark in the park but I managed to see the attacker. He had red hair and was wearing a V-neck sweater and baggy blue jeans.' The police immediately arrested Thomas on suspicion of kidnapping his own brother. What made them suspect him?

PUZZLE 81: WORD SWIRL

TIME LIMIT: 10 MINUTES

How many words of four or more letters can you make from the following word swirl?

Rules
1. Follow the clues below to find the word.
2. Each word must have the centre letter (G) in it.
3. All words have to be real words and not made up.

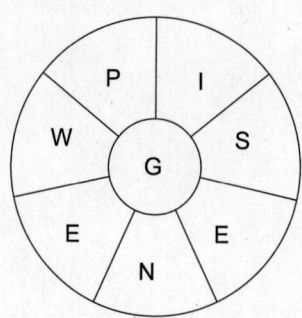

Clues
1. Stitching. (6 letters)
2. This comes out when Aladdin rubs a magic lamp. (5 letters)
3. In a playground, you can sit on this and move back and forth. (5 letters)
4. These help birds fly. (5 letters)
5. These farmyard animals live in a sty or pen. (4 letters)
6. A covering for the head made of real or artificial hair. (3 letters)
7. ____ ____ ____ ____ language is a language that uses gestures and hand signals. (4 letters)
8. To drink in large gulps. (4 letters)
9. Crying. (7 letters)
10. Can you figure out the 8-letter word? (**Hint:** It is something that you do to keep your house clean.)

Time taken: _____

PUZZLE 82: FOLDING CUBES   TIME LIMIT: 10 MINUTES

How many of the following cube nets can form three-dimensional cubes when they are folded?

Rules
1. Imagine that each shape is folded along its lines. You will have to manipulate the shapes in your mind and see which cube nets form cubes. If you find it hard to do this, trace or draw the shapes on a separate piece of paper and physically fold them on their lines to see if it makes a cube.
2. There should not be any overlapping flaps.

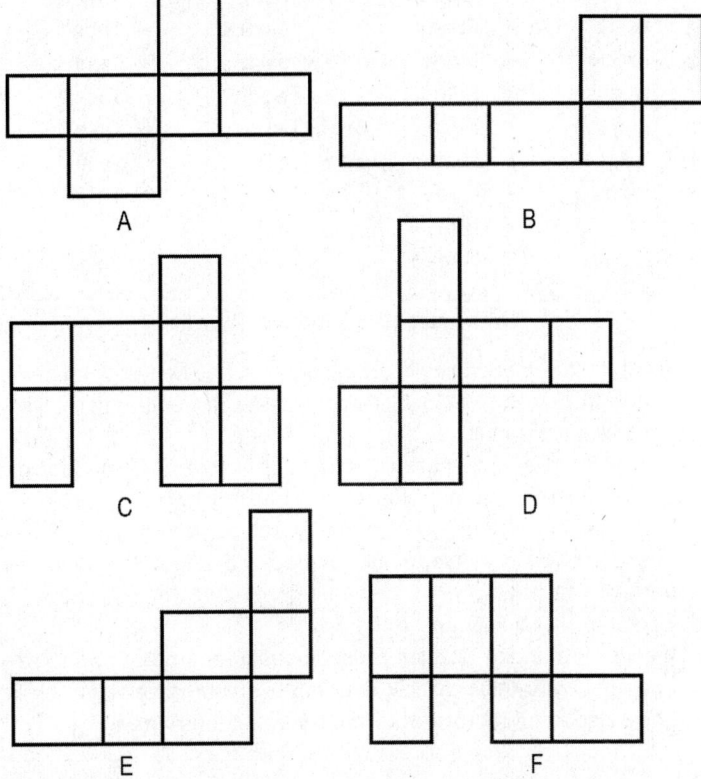

Time taken: _____

PUZZLE 83: WORD SEARCH–T

Find and circle the following words in the word search puzzle on the next page. All words begin with the letter T. The words can be found horizontally, vertically or diagonally, in any direction (back to front or bottom to top). There are 50 words to find in 30 minutes so try and find all the words as quickly as possible!

- Tactic
- Tables
- Taboo
- Tacked
- Tagged
- Tussle
- Tuxedo
- Tweaks
- Tugged
- Troll
- Tropes
- Trim
- Trauma
- Toucan
- Total
- Trousers
- Totem
- Tomato
- Toasty
- Today
- Tiffin
- Timing
- Thorny
- Three
- Thrift
- Thread
- Thanks
- Thrown
- Theme
- Theory
- Tent
- Teacups
- Tasks
- Twenty
- Taper
- Tasty
- Twist
- Truly
- Truth
- Trove
- Tromp
- Truce
- Trade
- Tray
- Tribe
- Tomb
- Tango
- Tone
- Tenth
- Threw

Fun Facts: Word Search Puzzles

- Word search was originally a Spanish puzzle. The first word search puzzle in English was published on 1 March 1968—after which it became very popular.
- Not all word search puzzles include a word list. Some just give you a general topic and you need to find the words yourself.
- Word search puzzles boost memory and brain health.
- These puzzles can keep your mind so active that they help keep dementia at bay.
- Each puzzle usually has a theme.
- Working out these puzzles reduces stress and helps you relax.
- They help you think quickly and improve your observation skills.
- They also help improve your concentration and focus.

TIME LIMIT: 30 MINUTES

T	A	G	G	E	D	T	E	E	R	H	T	W	E	A	K	S	V	T	N	T	J
A	X	T	Z	T	H	R	E	A	D	Q	I	H	T	U	R	T	I	R	N	W	L
C	D	R	N	O	T	O	T	T	F	J	F	C	O	R	D	M	C	A	W	E	O
T	O	U	C	A	N	V	O	U	D	T	F	T	N	B	I	C	N	U	O	N	O
I	V	C	C	S	E	E	M	G	X	H	I	S	E	N	L	M	Y	M	R	T	B
C	V	E	P	T	T	B	A	G	G	E	N	E	G	A	B	L	V	A	H	Y	A
T	A	S	T	Y	D	V	T	E	T	M	D	P	T	S	U	V	J	K	T	F	T

O	D	H	E	F	O	D	R
G	T	E	R	T	R	T	E
P	A	O	E	H	T	H	S
M	N	R	P	R	O	T	U
O	G	Y	A	E	M	O	O
R	O	N	T	W	B	D	R
T	C	D	E	K	C	A	T
E	T	R	I	B	E	Y	J
N	S	Q	T	A	S	K	S
T	K	V	R	F	V	T	B
H	N	C	O	T	T	R	Y
T	A	B	L	E	S	A	N
H	H	M	L	A	I	D	R
R	T	E	Y	C	W	E	O
I	R	T	R	U	T	R	H
F	A	O	H	P	C	F	T
T	Y	T	U	S	S	L	E

Time taken: _____

PUZZLE 84: SLITHERLINKS

The objective of this puzzle is to use the numbers inside the squares as guides to help you draw horizontal or vertical 'fences' around the entire puzzle to form a simple loop with no open ends. The numbers 1, 2 and 3 inside the squares represent the number of fences or loops around that particular number. This puzzle requires pure logic to solve and does not involve any guess work.

Rules
1. The fence or loop has to be a single continuous line throughout the puzzle. All line segments must be connected.
2. The loop cannot touch or cross itself at any point. It also cannot be left open at any point.
3. The number of fences around a particular number should correspond to that number. For example, if the number is 2, then only two fences can be drawn around that number, either to the left, right, top or bottom of the number.
4. If there is no number in a square, you can draw any number of lines surrounding that square in order to connect the loop to numbered squares.

Hints
1. If the number of fences surrounding a square correspond to the number in the square, all other possible horizontal and vertical lines surrounding that square can be eliminated.
2. Start with a number which points to a definite fence. For example, if there is a 3 in the corner, you know for sure that the two outside edges need to be drawn. That leaves only the two inside edges, which can be deduced using the other numbers surrounding it.

Example:

TIME LIMIT: 20 MINUTES

A)

		2	3	3	3	2	0		
0		2		1		2			
1		2		1		0	2	1	
3	2		2	3	1				2
	2	3		1	0				3
2	0	1				0			3
2		0				1			3
2	1	1	0	1			1		
3		3	3	2	1		0		

B)

3	2	2	2		1		2	2
2		1		0			3	3
2			1			1	2	
2		2	1	2			1	2
2		1	0		1		1	2
3	2		1	2		1	2	
2		2				1	2	1
		2	3	3		0		2
2	2	1		1	2	1		2

Time taken: _____

PUZZLE 85: FOODIE REVERSE CROSSWORD

In reverse crossword, all the answers are already given. You just need to place each answer in its correct slot. This puzzle requires pure logic to solve and does not involve any guesswork. Fit all the food and food-related words into their correct boxes.

Hint
Start with the word that you know will definitely fit into its correct slot and work your way around the crossword puzzle from there.

10-letter words
Cheesecake
Sauerkraut

8-letter words
Hazelnut
Macaroon
Meringue
Popsicle
Zucchini

7-letter words
Biscuit
Legumes
Ravioli
Sausage

6-letter words
Banana
Fennel
Ginger
Kiwano
Lentil
Raisin
Salami
Samosa

5-letter words
Guava
Mochi
Pecan
Sushi

4-letter words
Amla (indian gooseberry)
Bran
Eggs
Feta
Kiwi
Lime
Milk
Mint
Pita
Rice
Taco

3-letter words
Jam
Mug
Nut
Pie
Soy
Wok

TIME LIMIT: 10 MINUTES

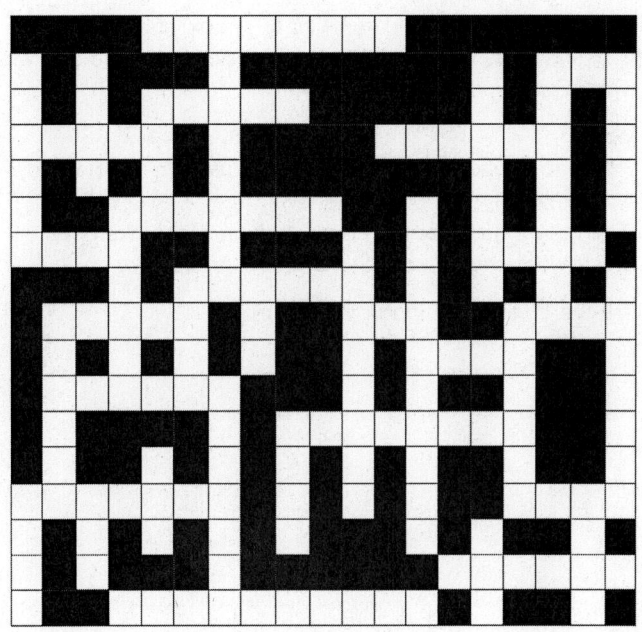

Time taken: _____

Bonus Game: Anagrams

An anagram is a word that can be formed by rearranging the letters of another word. For example, LOOPED is an anagram of POODLE. Find the anagram for the words that are the capital letters.

1. He held the LAMP in the ___ ___ ___ ___ of his hand.
2. He got FIRED because his ___ ___ ___ ___ ___ chicken tasted horrible.
3. She had to STUDY from the ___ ___ ___ ___ ___ old books.
4. He put some LEMON on the ___ ___ ___ ___ ___ to add some taste to it.
5. He gave her a RING with a big ___ ___ ___ ___ on his face.

PUZZLE 86: WORD PYRAMID

TIME LIMIT: 10 MINUTES

Beginning at the top, add a letter to a box at each step, moving towards the bottom seven-letter word. Solve each clue and write the answer in each corresponding row.

Rules
1. The same letter or letters should be used in the next row—plus an additional letter.
2. The letters may be rearranged to form a new word.
3. Each word should correspond to the given clue.

Follow the clues to fill in the word pyramid.

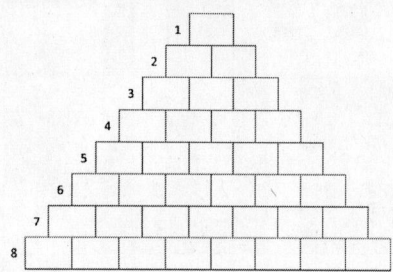

Clues
1. Me, myself and ___.
2. She ___ ___ going to school.
3. A polite, respectful way of addressing a man, especially one in a position of authority.
4. The sun will ___ ___ ___ ___ at 6 am tomorrow.
5. An alarm bell or warning bell that makes a long, prolonged sound.
6. The king ___ ___ ___ ___ ___ ___ (rules) over the country.
7. Another word for a vocalist (plural).
8. A bandage used to cover and protect a wound can also be called a ___ ___ ___ ___ ___ ___ ___ ___.

Time taken: _____

Bonus Puzzle: Code Decode

A police detective received a baffling note from a murderer informing him of where his next murders would be committed. The note read 'Solo pairs hasten avenge'. The detective immediately mobilized the police force in various cities. Can you decipher the note?

PUZZLE 87: LOOPY LOOPS

TIME LIMIT: 20 MINUTES

Draw a single loop that passes through the centre of every white square using only horizontal and vertical lines. The loop cannot pass through any square more than once, cannot cross itself or pass through any of the black squares.

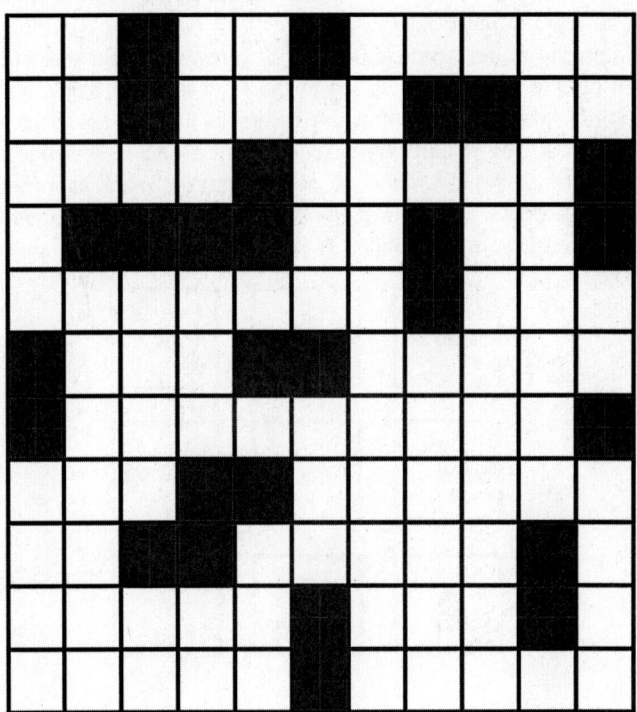

Time taken: _____

Riddle Me This

I can be all colours
Or no colour at all,
Sometimes I'm half empty,
At others, half full.
What am I?

PUZZLE 88: WHAT COMES NEXT?

Look at the sequences of tiles below and logically work out what answer should fit into the blank box at the end. Try to work out the plan, scheme or order behind every row and column of tiles. Choose your answer from options A to E. Each question may require a different kind of logic to solve it.

Looking at the example below, going row-wise, we see that each black square moves one space to the right in each block while the black dot keeps moving from the centre to the left and back to the centre. The grey square starts at the centre and moves one space to the right. Going column-wise, we see that the black square moves one space down, while the black dot and grey square remain in the same place. Therefore, Option B would fit into the empty space.

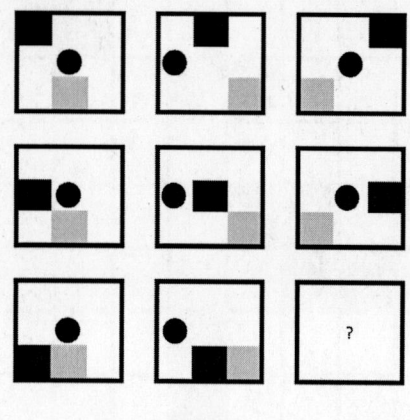

Options:

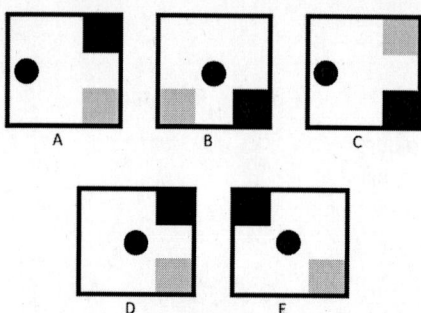

TIME LIMIT: 10 MINUTES

The first three rows are related in some way. Find the fourth row from Options A to E.

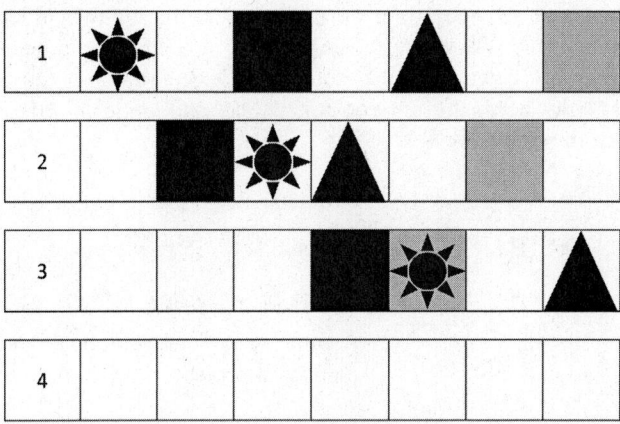

Options:

Time taken: _____

PUZZLE 89: WORD SQUARES

TIME LIMIT: 10 MINUTES

Word squares consist of a set of words written in a grid in such a way that the same words can be read both horizontally and vertically. The number of words is generally equal to the number of letters in each word. All the words cross perfectly in a square arrangement.

You are given clues that correspond to the rows. All you need to do is write down the answer horizontally and vertically to complete the word square.

Example:

T	O	P	I	C	The subject of a conversation.
O	C	H	R	E	A pale brown yellow colour.
P	H	A	I	L	A small cylindrical glass bottle used for medical samples.
I	R	A	T	E	Annoyed.
C	E	L	E	B	Slang for famous person.

Work out the word square below:

					A grown up person.
					Currency used in Algeria, Bahrain, Iraq, Jordan, Kuwait, Libya etc.
					Bring together.
					A type of coffee made with espresso and lots of milk.
					'You can't see the forest for the ___ ___ ___ ___ ___.'

Time taken: _____

Bonus Game: Word Finder

Find at least **ten** 4-letter words in the word scramble below. Can you also find the word that uses up all 8 letters?

A	I	R	M	A	L	E	T

PUZZLE 90: WORD CIRCLES

TIME LIMIT: 10 MINUTES

Given below are nine-letter words arranged in circles. They are not jumbled. Find the correct word and write it down. The words can be read clockwise or counterclockwise.

1. O N
    D   E
    N   D
    A B A

Answer: _____

2. S P
    B   I
    A   L
    C K F

Answer: _____

3. U S
    O   D
    R   A
    E G N

Answer: _____

4. R A
    E   T
    N   E
    E G D

Answer: _____

5. O L
    O   B
    H   A
    C S G

Answer: _____

Time taken: _____

6. I E
    T   S
    I   A
    L I B

Answer: _____

7. A C
    P   Y
    T   T
    I V I

Answer: _____

8. A O
    R   B
    D   H
    D A S

Answer: _____

9. R R
    A   E
    I   T
    N W A

Answer: _____

10. E T
    N   E
    O   L
    H P E

Answer: _____

PUZZLE 91: REVERSE MINESWEEPER

Reverse minesweeper is a puzzle that begins with all the answers revealed. You will need to place mines around the number squares. The number of mines around a number square corresponds to the number of the square. For example, if the number is 2, it indicates that there are two mines in the immediate squares that surround it.

Rules
1. Place a mine into the empty squares that surround each number, including diagonally adjacent squares. You can either draw a mine or shade the cell to represent the mine.
2. The number of mines around a number needs to correspond to the value of the number.

Hints
1. There may be blank squares as well. Mark these off with an X so that you don't get confused.
2. Start with a square that you know for sure is a mine.

Look at the example given below to get an idea of the completed puzzle.

●		●			●	2		4	●
3	4		1	1			●	●	●
●	●	1		1			3		
2		1	0		●	2	●		0
				2					
	●	1		●	2		●		
	1					●	2		0
	1		0		●	2	2	1	
●	2			2				●	
●	2		●			0			1

TIME LIMIT: 10 MINUTES

Place 20 mines in the puzzle below.

1	1						2	
2			0	0				
							0	
	3	0			4		2	
			2			2		0
			2		2			0
0						2	3	
		2		1	1			3
	2	0		0			4	
					0			3

Time taken: _____

Bonus: Rebus Puzzle

A rebus puzzle is a picture representation of a common word, saying or phrase. For example, /R/E/A/D/I/N/G/ could be interpreted as 'Reading between the lines'. Try and solve the following Rebus puzzles.

1.	2.	3.	4.
TENT**BAD**IONS	BIG BIG IGNORE IGNORE	COME TABLE TABLE TABLE TABLE	R E E T T S

PUZZLE 92: MATCHING SHAPES TIME LIMIT: 10 MINUTES

Draw lines to match each identical shape. The lines must not cross each other or touch each other. There must never be more than one connecting line in any square. All lines have to be horizontal or vertical lines only. No diagonal lines are allowed. Look at the example given below to get an idea of the completed puzzle.

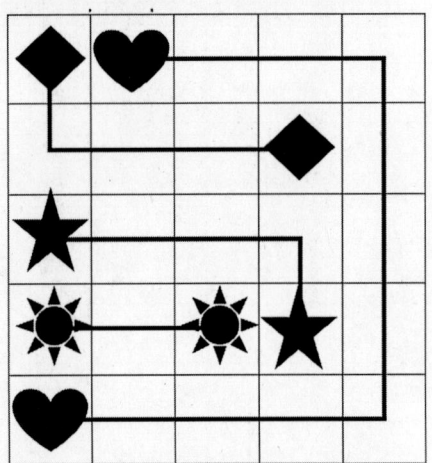

Now match the identical shapes in the figure below.

Time taken: _____

PUZZLE 93: TANGRAM   TIME LIMIT: 10 MINUTES

Using all seven tangram shapes from the beginning of the book, make the figure of the sitting man below. You can cut out the shapes from the book, trace the shapes on a different sheet of paper and cut them out, or use Tangram blocks, if you have them.

Rules
1. All seven pieces must be used.
2. All seven pieces must touch each other.
3. None of the pieces should overlap.

Time taken: _____

Bonus Puzzle: Counting Squares

How many squares are there in this picture?

PUZZLE 94: DIVIDING SHAPES

Divide the following figure into equal parts by drawing along the lines of the inner squares.

Rules
1. Each of the divided shapes should be identical to each other.
2. There should be no added or left out squares.
3. If all divided parts are rotated to face the same direction, they should all be exactly the same size and look exactly alike.

Hint
Count the squares inside the figure and divide the total by the total required. This will give you an idea of how many squares are needed inside the figure.

In the following example, the figure needs to be divided by **three** equal parts.

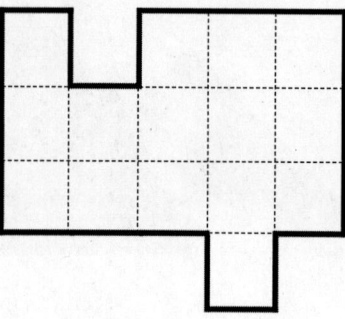

Answer:

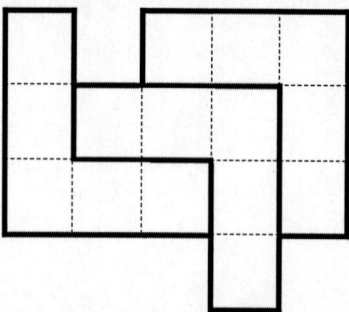

TIME LIMIT: 10 MINUTES

A) Divide the following figure into **six** equal parts.

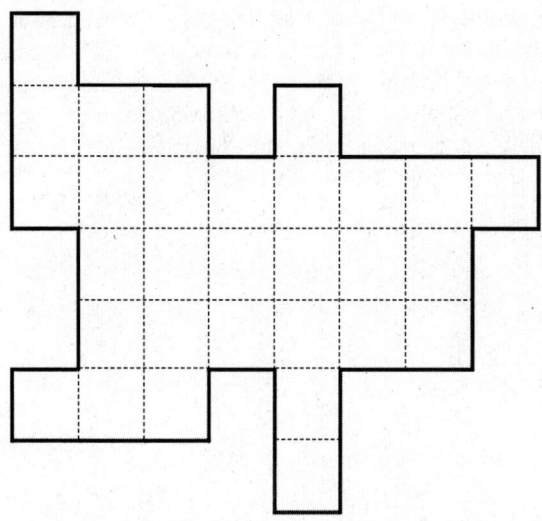

B) Divide the following figure into **seven** equal parts.

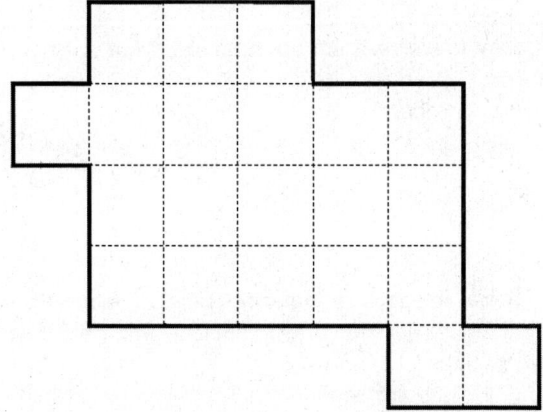

Time taken: _____

PUZZLE 95: CODE DECODE
TIME LIMIT: 20 MINUTES

Morse code was developed by Samuel Morse in the 1840s to send messages over the electric telegraph that he invented in 1836. The idea was that the electrical signals would punch marks on paper tapes in either dots or dashes. Today, Morse code is used only for navigational radio beacons, amateur radio operators and land mobile transmitter identification. Here are the letters for Morse code. Use them to decipher the sentences below.

(**Hint:** The forward slash (/) depicts spaces between words.)

A: .-	G: --.	M: --	S: ...	Y: -.--
B: -...	H:	N: -.	T: -	Z: --..
C: -.-.	I: ..	O: ---	U: ..-	
D: -..	J: .---	P: .--.	V: ...-	
E: .	K: -.-	Q: --.-	W: .--	
F: ..-.	L: .-..	R: .-.	X: -..-	

1. Common nursery rhyme.
   -- .- .-. -.- /.... .- -../.-/.-.. .. - - -.. ./.-.. .- - - -...
2. A term used to describe a person who is lazing around.
   -.-. --- ..- -.-. ..../.- -. --- - .-- --- ---
3. A distress signal.
   ... - - - ...
4. I am easy to waste. I am unstoppable. What am I?
   Answer: - .. -- .
5. A popular childhood game
   .... --- .-. ... . -.-. --- - -.-. ....

Time taken: _____

Bonus Puzzle: Code Decode

A suitcase lock needs to be opened with 3 numbers in the correct order. Try to figure out the correct combination for the lock based on the following clues.

1. **387**: All digits are wrong
2. **781**: One digit is right and in its right place.
3. **836**: One digit is right but in the wrong place.
4. **197**: Two digits are right but both are in the wrong place
5. **983**: One digit is right and in the right place.

PUZZLE 96: COUNTING CUBES

TIME LIMIT: 5 MINUTES

Count the cubes in the image below. Keep in mind that this image is in 3D and there may be some cubes that you cannot see.

(**Hint:** Don't forget to count the cubes that are hidden behind or beneath the cubes that you can see.)

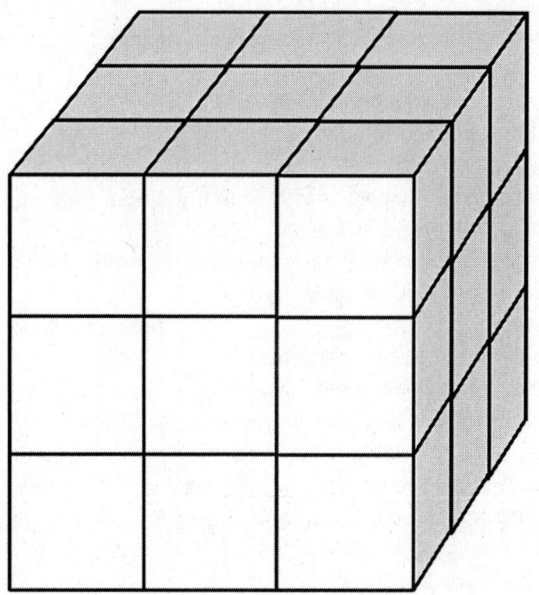

Time taken: _____

Riddle Me This

I look very sorry
When you're feeling sad,
And I look happy,
When you're feeling glad.
What am I?

PUZZLE 97: CROSSWORD SCHOOL

The following crossword puzzle involves all the people and things that are associated with a school. Solve the clues to complete the crossword puzzle.

Across
2. Your teacher writes with chalk on a _____.
4. A building in your school that contains books that you can read and borrow.
6. A person who teaches is called a _____.
7. Another word for students.
9. You can write or draw on a sheet of _____.
12. An assignment or piece of research that can be done individually or in a group and submitted.
14. Creative activity resulting in the production of paintings, drawings, or sculpture is also known as _____.
16. We study from a _____ and a notebook for each subject.
18. Do you need to sharpen your _____?
19. A folder that holds loose papers together.
21. Something that can help you draw straight lines.
24. When you are taking a test and you have to say the answer out loud, it is said to be an _____ test.
25. A large hall in school, generally used for morning assembly and functions.
27. These come in different colours and you can write with them.
28. Which subject studies the physical features of the earth and its atmosphere?
29. The classmates that you like and hang out with in school are your _____.
30. Which subject studies past events?

Down
1. Short form of gymnasiums
2. When parents need to go to work, they can leave their children at day_____.
3. Your school bag can also be called a _____.
5. Generally, a sheet of paper that contains all the marks of a student is called a _____ card.
8. Chemistry, Physics and Biology are all _____ subjects.
10. I am _____ a very sad book right now.

11. Full form of Maths.
12. The head of your school is called the _____.
13. Short form of laboratory.
15. She won the _____ bee competition last year.
17. A piece of clothing worn around the neck, usually as part of 22 down.
20. He drew a bar_____, a pie _____ and a flow_____ to illustrate his point.
22. The similar clothes that you and your classmates wear, that also denote which school you attend.
23. School work that you do at home is called _____.
26. An open ground where Physical Education classes may take place.

TIME LIMIT: 20 MINUTES

Time taken: _____

PUZZLE 98: HASHI TIME LIMIT: 20 MINUTES

Connect all islands with bridges.

Rules
1. The number of bridges coming in and going out from each island needs to be the same as the number on the island.
2. You can only draw horizontal and vertical lines to connect islands. No diagonal lines are allowed.
3. Bridges cannot cut across each other or any of the islands.
4. You can draw one line to represent one bridge.
5. There cannot be more than two bridges for each pair of islands (although there can be more bridges leading away from the island to a different island). The total number of bridges per island can be anywhere from one to eight, depending on the number on the island.
6. All islands must be connected so that if you start at one island, you should be able to travel to every other island using the bridges.

Hint
Start with an island where you know for sure which direction the bridges go. For example, you can start with Island 1 on the first, third, fifth and sixth rows.

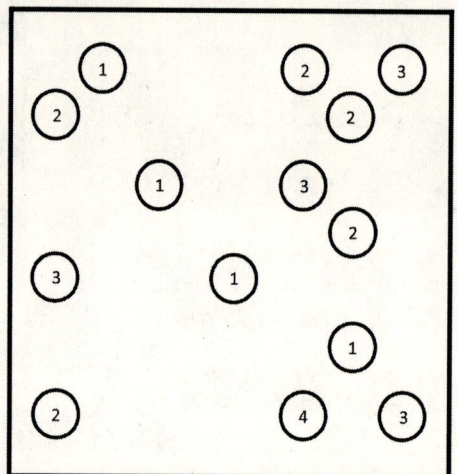

Time taken: _____

PUZZLE 99: LETTER SLIDES

TIME LIMIT: 10 MINUTES

Letter slides are formed by starting at one letter and sliding your way to a connecting letter to form a word. Solve the clues below to find words.

Rules
1. Words can be formed only by sliding from one letter to another letter that is either above, below, to the left, to the right or diagonally. You cannot skip letters to reach another letter.
2. You cannot use the same letter more than once in any word.

P	I	N	E	I
H	S	D	F	R

Clues
A) One of the primary colours. (3 letters)
B) You can put this out with water. (4 letters)
C) Another word for a backbone. (5 letters)
D) A type of evergreen tree that has __ __ __ __ cones. (4 letters)
E) The dog has forelegs and __ __ __ __ legs. (4 letters)
F) He __ __ __ __ his paintbrush into water to clean it. (4 letters)
G) A body part near the pelvis that you can possibly dislocate. (3 letters)
H) Food that is cooked in hot oil is said to be __ __ __ __ __. (5 letters)
I) __ __ __ __ and Seek. (4 letters)
J) Can you figure out the 10-letter word? **Hint:** Start with the letter F.

Time taken: _____

Bonus Puzzle: First and Last

Find the first two letters and the last two letters of each word. (**Hint:** The last two letters of each word are the first two letters of the next word.)

A	P	P	R	O	A		
		A	I	R	M		
		N	O	U	N		
		L	L	U	L		
		T	I	S	T		

PUZZLE 100: MATH WHIZ

TIME LIMIT: 10 MINUTES

Solve the following mathematical links to get your final answer. Try to solve them in your head without writing anything down or using a calculator. Just follow the links downwards and solve the mathematical instructions given in each link. Once you have the answer, move to the next link below.

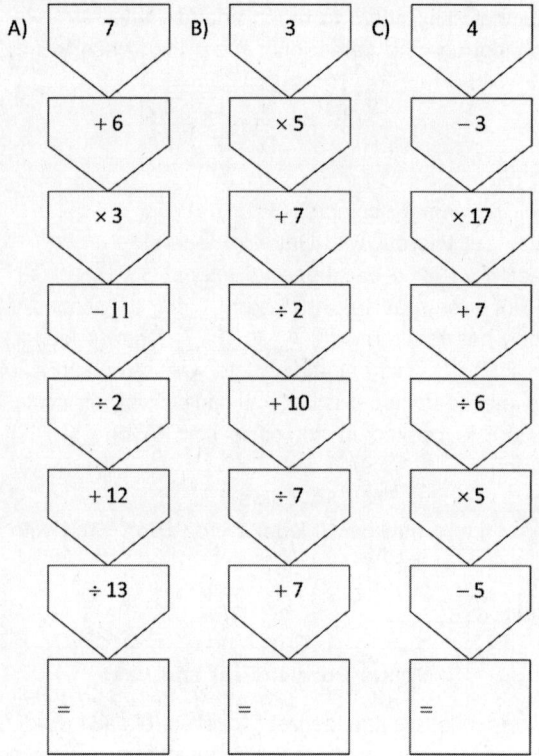

Time taken: _____

What Comes Next?

Look at the sequence of numbers below and try to figure out what number should replace the question mark.

1, 2, 3, 5, 8, 13, 21, ?

WHAT MORE CAN YOU DO?

Logical and Analytical Thinking
Now that you have completed this book of logic puzzles, you may notice that your concentration and focus have increased, your mind has become sharper, you are able to solve problems in a more logical and analytical way and your memory power is much stronger than before. But don't stop here! You can continue to hone these skills by following some of the suggestions below.

- If you liked a particular type of puzzle in this book, look out for other books or websites with similar puzzles and continue working them out.
- Keep timing yourself when you do puzzles and try to beat your previous record. This improves your concentration and focus.
- Try and make your own brain games, brain teasers and puzzles. Use existing formats and try and find variations for them. For example, the reverse crossword and reverse minesweeper puzzles that you solved in this book are variations of the classic crossword and minesweeper puzzles. Making up your own puzzles will also sharpen your mind.
- Keep trying new activities that are varied and different from each other but require just one solution. Crocheting, cross-stitch, knitting patterns and other forms of embroidery are just a few examples of these activities.
- Games such as Clue, Risk, Chess, Chinese Checkers, Settlers of Catan, Mancala, Pandemic, Mastermind, Monopoly, Prime Climb, etc. require strategy, analysis and critical thinking. Other games such as Scrabble and Boggle help you analyze information quickly.
- Certain card games such as Free Cell also require some amount of strategy and planning. These games are available online.
- Take at least ten minutes to half an hour out of your day to solve logic puzzles such as Sudoku, Kakuro, Hanjie, Futoshiki, Calcudoku, Hitori, Slitherlink, Skyscraper, Nurikabe, etc.
- Make mathematics fun. Logic and analytical thinking play a huge role in mathematics. You can challenge yourself by playing maths games on various websites and mobile applications.
- Learn a musical instrument. While this may seem more like an art, you require hard logic to follow timing, read music and translate

that music to specific finger movements on a keyboard, guitar or other instruments.
- Solve mysteries and break codes. Reading crime stories and detective novels requires logical and analytical thinking on the part of the reader. Breaking codes and solving riddles as a hobby also helps keep your brain razor sharp. Try making up unique codes that only you and your friends can decipher. Try a Mystery Room with your friends.
- Look at everyday problems from a logical perspective and take a problem-solving approach while solving them. Most problems in our daily lives can be solved logically and practically. When we allow ourselves to get emotional about some problems, we take a longer time to deal with them and this can lead to overwhelming stress. This stress can be either avoided or reduced substantially by dealing with the problem logically.
- Try to avoid making assumptions in daily situations. It would be best to stick to facts as much as possible. Rather than reacting to everyday problems, try taking the time to analyze them and respond to them logically. Take the time to read situations rather than react to them. This will reduce the overall stress in your life.

As mentioned earlier, solving puzzles helps keep your brain sharp; so try and make this a lifelong activity. Above all, remember to have fun!

ANSWERS

Puzzle 1: Maze Amaze

Puzzle 2: Word Ladders

A)

R	U	G
H	U	G
H	A	G
H	A	T

B)

T	E	A
P	E	A
P	E	T
P	U	T
P	U	P
C	U	P

Puzzle 3: Domino Twist

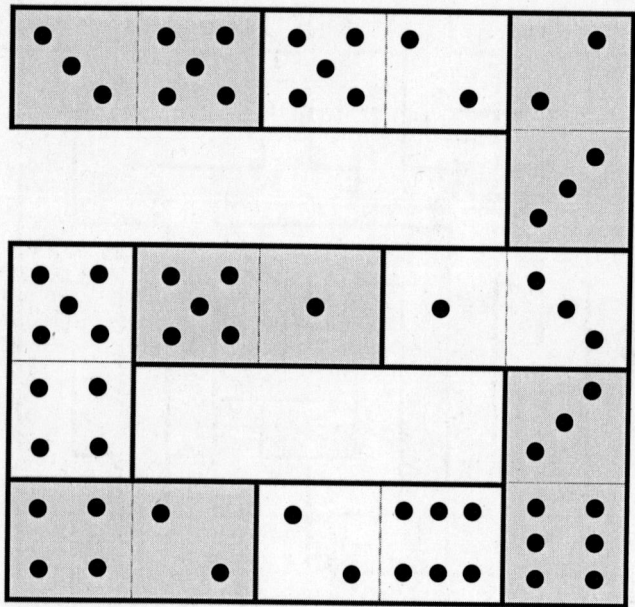

Puzzle 4: Mini Sudoku

A)	4	2	1	3
	3	1	4	2
	1	3	2	4
	2	4	3	1

B)	4	1	3	2
	2	3	4	1
	1	4	2	3
	3	2	1	4

Fun Activity: Thinking outside the box

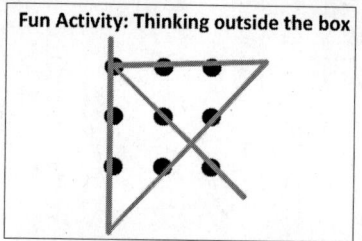

Puzzle 5: Coin Board

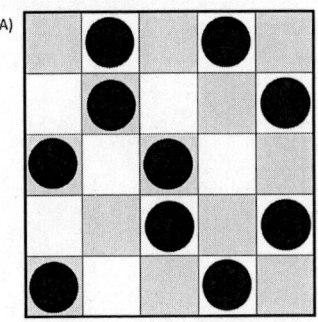
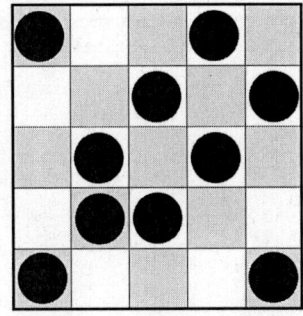

Bonus Game: Coin Touch

Arrange three coins touching each other at the bottom and one coin at the top like this:

Puzzle 6: Word Swirl

1. Claus
2. Places
3. Capes
4. Cause
5. Space
6. Clap
7. Laces
8. Scale
9. Clues
10. Capsule

Puzzle 7: Folding Cubes
Shapes D, F, H, J, N and P can be folded to form cubes.

Puzzle 8: Word Search– P

Fun Activity: Thinking outside the box

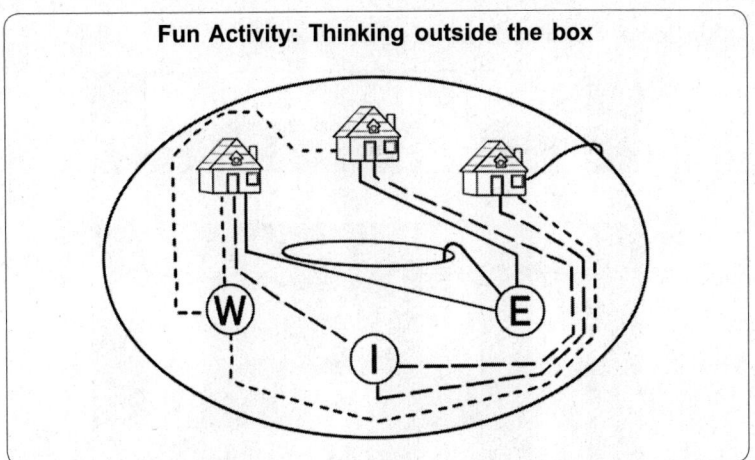

Puzzle 9: Slitherlinks

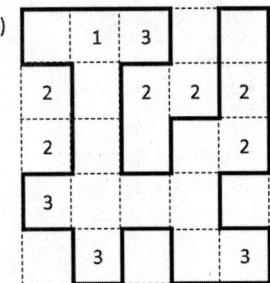

Puzzle 10: Happiness Reverse Crossword

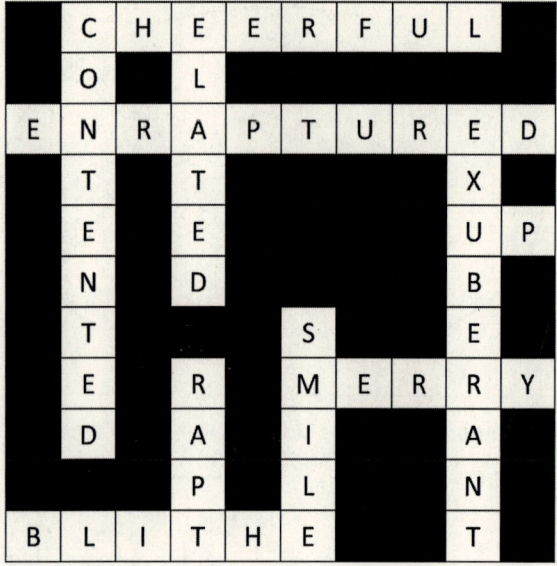

Puzzle 11: Word Pyramid

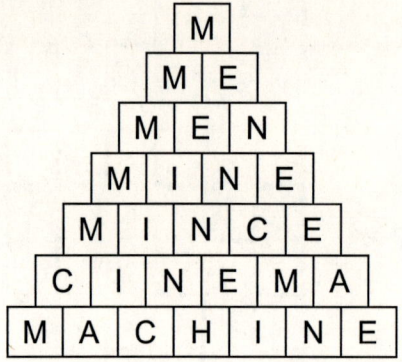

Word Unscramble: Hidden Animals

1. Giraffe
2. Zebra
3. Elephant

Puzzle 12: Loopy Loops

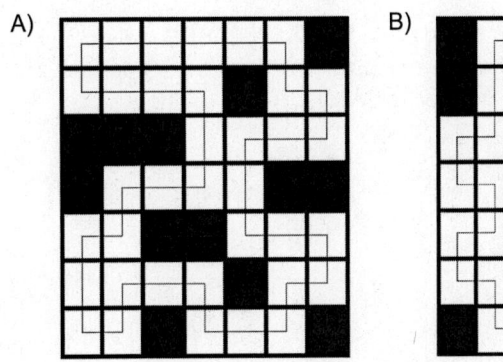

Riddle Me This

Sarah has five children. Each daughter has the same brother.

Puzzle 13: What Comes Next?

Option E is the correct answer. Going row-wise, both black circles move one space to the right. Since the right black circle has no space to move right, it starts from the top again. Going column-wise, both black circles move one space down. Since the left black circle cannot move down by another space, it starts at the top again.

Brain Teaser: Add word

HOUSE (Clubhouse, Farmhouse, Warehouse)

Puzzle 14: Word Squares

A)

A	C	E
C	A	T
E	T	C

B)

B	A	B	Y
A	R	E	A
B	E	A	N
Y	A	N	K

Reasoning Puzzle

They finished eating chocolate in this order: CABDE. A finished before B but after C, so the order is CAB. We know that D finished before E but after B, so the order is CABDE.

Puzzle 15: Word Circles

1. Cannot
2. Inside
3. Reward/Drawer
4. Wholly
5. Unlike
6. Former
7. Module
8. Signed
9. Valley
10. Victim

Puzzle 16: Reverse Minesweeper

A)

1	💣	3	2		0
	3	💣	💣		
2	💣		4	💣	2
3	💣			💣	3
💣	3	2		💣	3
	💣	1	2	💣	2

B)

	1		0	1	1	1
1	💣				💣	2
		3	💣	💣	4	💣
💣	2	4	💣			1
3			💣		0	
💣	💣	2		2		
2	2		1	💣	1	0

Riddle Me This

The man was bald. Therefore, not a 'single hair on his head' got wet.

Puzzle 17: Matching Shapes

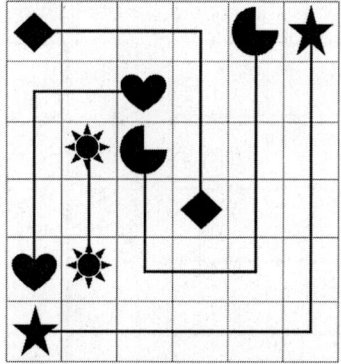

Puzzle 18: Tangram

Brain Teaser: Add Word

SUN (Sunburn, Sunspot, Sunbeam)

Puzzle 19: Dividing Shapes
You can either divide the square horizontally or vertically.

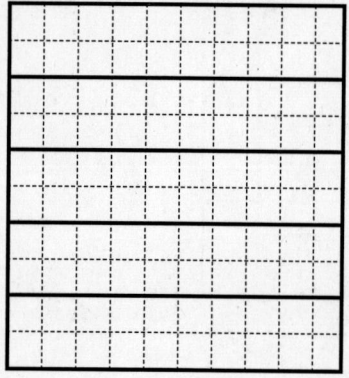 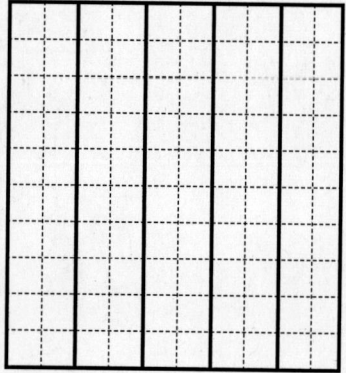

Bonus Puzzle

The letter A.

Puzzle 20: Code Decode
A) Practice makes perfect. (Shift by one letter)
B) Beggars can't be choosers. (Shift by three letters)
C) As you sow, so shall you reap. (Shift by five letters)

Puzzle 21: Counting Cubes
17 cubes– 9 on the bottom row, 5 on the middle row and 3 on the top row.

Riddle Me This

A clock!

Puzzle 22: Crossword Farm

Bonus: Rebus Puzzle

1. Try to understand.
2. Travel overseas.
3. What goes up must come down.
4. Forgive (four give) and forget (four get).

Puzzle 23: Hashi

A)

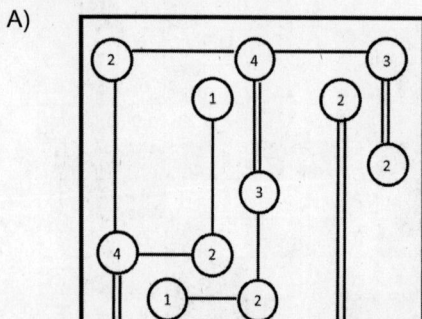

B)

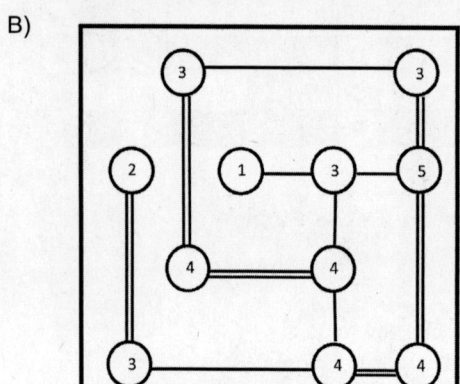

Puzzle 24: Letter Slides

A) Baking
B) King
C) Rake
D) Beg
E) Begin

F) Bag
G) Rag
H) Gab
I) Nike
J) Breaking

Puzzle 25: Math Whiz

A) 13
B) 4
C) 2

Puzzle 26: Maze Amaze

Puzzle 27: Word Ladders

A)
F	O	O	T
B	O	O	T
B	O	L	T
B	E	L	T
B	E	L	L
B	A	L	L

B)
F	I	R	E
H	I	R	E
H	E	L	T
H	E	R	D
H	E	A	D
H	E	A	T

Bonus Game: Assembling a Word Square

M	I	N	D
I	D	E	A
N	E	A	T
D	A	T	A

Puzzle 28: Domino Twist

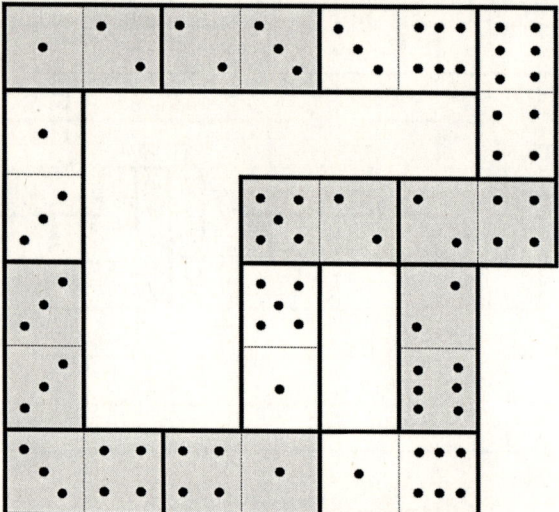

Puzzle 29: Mini Sudoku

A)

3	5	6	1	4	2
4	2	1	5	6	3
2	3	4	6	1	5
1	6	5	2	3	4
5	1	3	4	2	6
6	4	2	3	5	1

B)

2	3	1	4	5	6
4	5	6	1	3	2
5	6	4	2	1	3
1	2	3	6	4	5
3	1	2	5	6	4
6	4	5	3	2	1

Riddle Me This

Empty.

Puzzle 30: Coin Board (possible solutions)

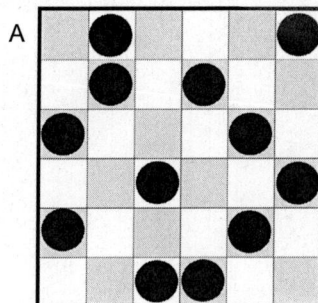
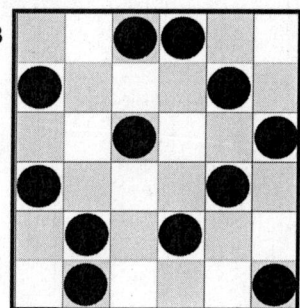

Bonus Game: Anagrams

1. Sobs
2. Tone
3. Eat
4. Who
5. Save

Puzzle 31: Word Swirl

1. Dad
2. Ads
3. Red
4. Dead
5. Read
Bonus– Address

6. Sad
7. Dress
8. Dare
9. Adder
10. Sadder

Puzzle 32: Folding Cubes

Cube nets C, E and F can be folded into cubes.

Puzzle 33: Word Search– O

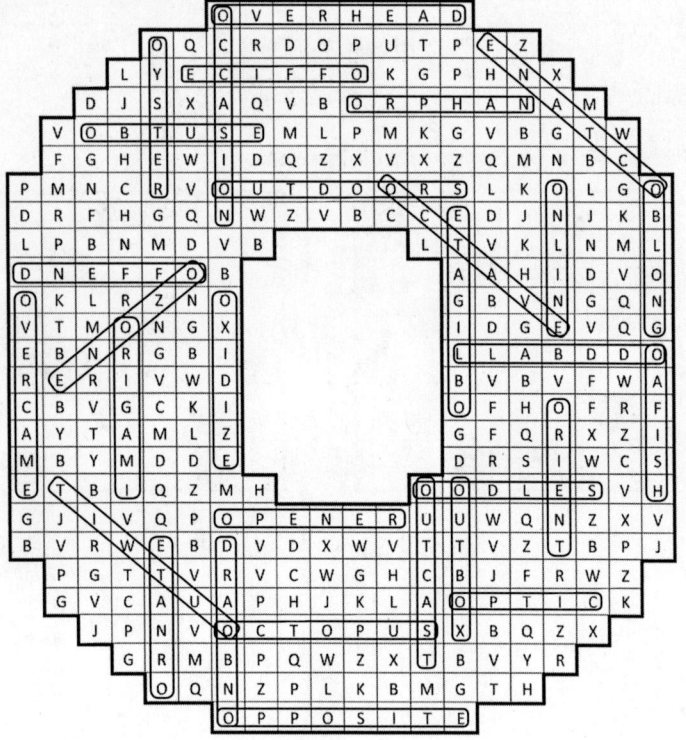

Bonus: Above/Below

F	D	G
I	A	C
B	H	E

Puzzle 34: Slitherlinks

> **Riddle Me This**
>
> Friday. The 'day before tomorrow' is today; 'the day before two days after' is really one day after. So if 'one day after today is Saturday', then today must be Friday.

Puzzle 35: Mythical Creatures Reverse Crossword

D	R	A	K	O	N			A	M	A	L	A
I			U				P		I			D
R			M		S	P	H	I	N	X		R
A			I				O		O			O
W			H				E		T			A
O		G	O	B	L	I	N		A			N
N		H					I		U			Z
G		O			M		X		R			I
		U			E						G	
		L	E	P	R	E	C	H	A	U	N	S
					M		Y				O	
	H	Y	D	R	A		C			I	M	P
					I		L		T	E		
F		O		D		O	G	R	E	S		
A		N				P		O				
U	N	I	C	O	R	N	S		O	L		
N								L	Y	N	X	

Puzzle 36: Word Pyramid

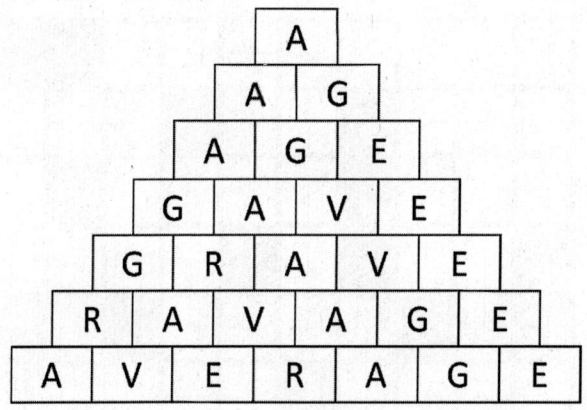

Logical thinking: Analogies

A frame covers a picture just as binding covers a book. Therefore, B is the correct answer.

Puzzle 37: Loopy Loops

Bonus: Rebus Puzzle

1. Scrambled eggs
2. Top secret
3. Eifel Tower
4. Jack in the box

Puzzle 38: What Comes Next?

Option D is the correct answer. Going row-wise, the first row plus the second row equals the third row. Going column-wise, with each column, the tiles rotate one space to the right.

Bonus Game: Odd One Out

Mummy is the odd one out. All the other words start and end with the same letters.

Puzzle 39: Word Squares

A)
O	M	I	T
M	A	D	E
I	D	E	A
T	E	A	M

B)
B	L	O	W
L	O	V	E
O	V	E	R
W	E	R	E

Puzzle 40: Word Circles

1. Gallery
2. Fishing
3. Printer
4. Welcome
5. Musical
6. Journey
7. Message
8. Studied
9. Reading
10. Schools

Puzzle 41: Reverse Minesweeper

A)

1		1		2	
	💣	2	1	💣	💣
3	💣		1	2	2
	💣	2	1	2	
2	2	1		💣	💣
💣	1		2	💣	3

B)

3	💣	2		1	3	💣
💣	💣	2		💣	4	💣
	2	1		2	💣	
	2	1	1		2	2
💣	2	💣		1	1	💣
1	2	3	💣	2		2
	0		💣			💣

> **Riddle Me This**
>
> Today!

Puzzle 42: Matching Shapes

Puzzle 43: Tangram

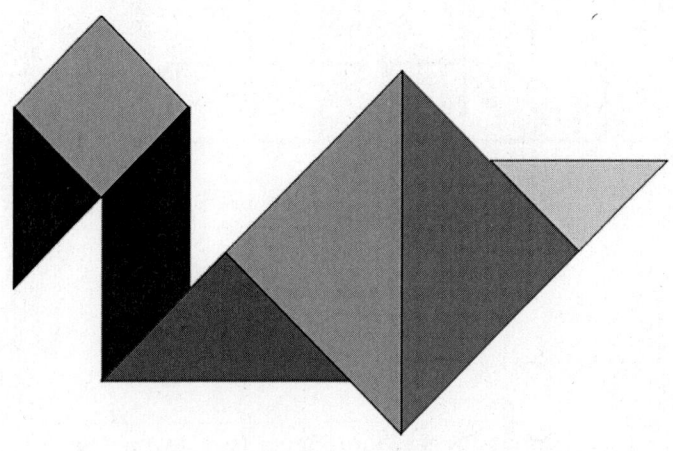

Bonus Game: Anagrams

1. Flow
2. Nails
3. Plum
4. Swell
5. Votes

Puzzle 44: Dividing Shapes

A)

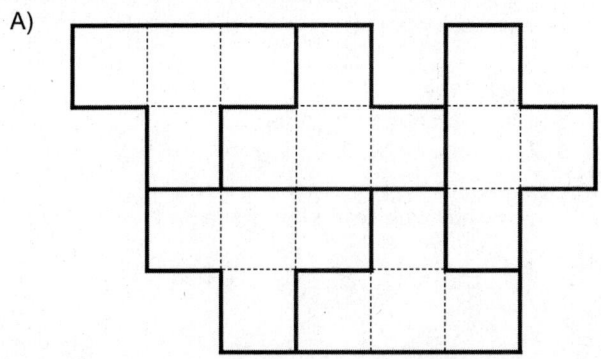

B)

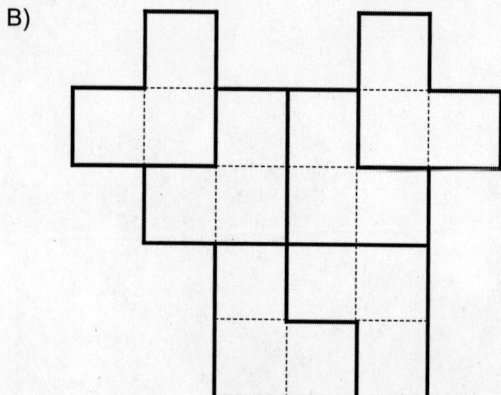

Bonus Game: Word Finder (possible words)

Deni, dens, desi, dies, dine, dins, dish, ends, feds, fend, fens, fids, find, fine, fins, fish, hens, hide, hied, hies, hind, hins, ides, nide, nidi, nisi, seif, send, shed, shen, shin, side, sine, sned.
8-Letter words: Finished and Fiendish

Puzzle 45: Code Decode
A) The wheels on the bus go round and round.
B) Zeus, Poseidon, Hades, Ares
C) Dawdle, Lounge, Dally, Laze, Rest
D) Queen, Duke, Emperor, Princess, Baron
E) Cold, Frosty, Icy, Snowing, Frozen

Puzzle 46: Counting Cubes
A) 8 cubes– 6 at the bottom and 2 on top.
B) 8 cubes– 5 at the bottom and 3 on top.

Bonus Puzzle: Letter Mash

The letter H.

Puzzle 47: Crossword Fairy Tale

Riddle Me This

A shoe!

Puzzle 48: Hashi

A)

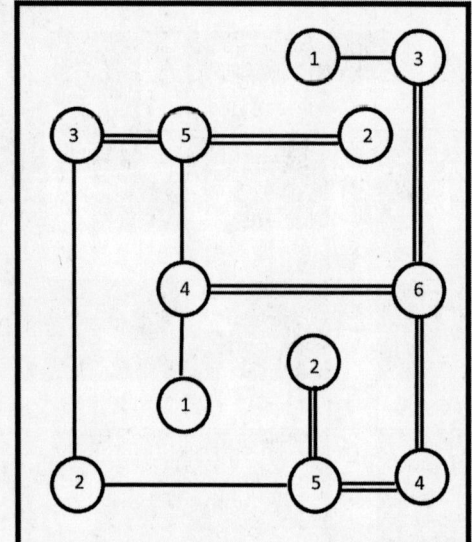

B)

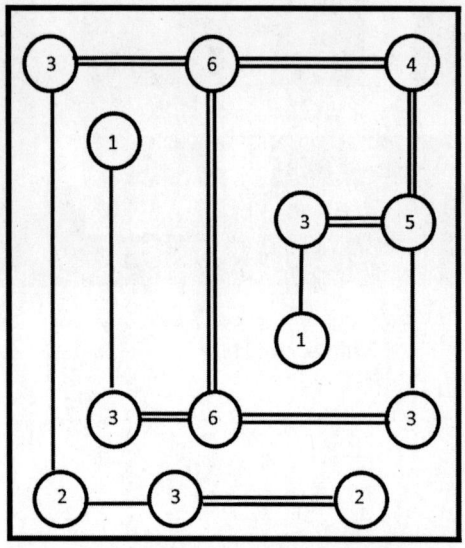

Puzzle 49: Letter Slides
A) Hop
B) Shop
C) Pita
D) Post
E) Pit
F) Spit
G) Lips
H) Sit
I) Tail
J) Hospital

Bonus Game: Opposites Attract

F	R	I	E	N	D
			N		
			E		
			M		
			Y		

Puzzle 50: Math Whiz
A) 100
B) 20
C) 30

What Comes Next?

19 comes next. Each number increases by 3.

Puzzle 51: Maze Amaze

Puzzle 52: Word Ladders

A)

N	A	M	E
D	A	M	E
D	A	M	S
D	I	M	S
A	I	M	S
A	R	M	S
A	R	M	Y

B)

L	I	O	N
L	O	O	N
L	O	O	T
L	O	U	T
L	O	U	D
L	O	A	D
T	O	A	D

Bonus Game: Assembling A Word Square

F	R	O	M
R	O	P	E
O	P	E	N
M	E	N	D

Puzzle 53: Domino Twist

Puzzle 54: Mini-Sudoku

A)

2	1	6	8	3	5	4	7
3	5	7	4	2	8	6	1
6	3	1	7	8	4	5	2
8	2	4	5	7	6	1	3
5	4	2	3	6	1	7	8
7	6	8	1	5	3	2	4
4	8	5	2	1	7	3	6
1	7	3	6	4	2	8	5

B)

1	2	3	7	6	8	4	5
8	5	6	4	1	7	2	3
4	8	1	2	5	3	7	6
6	7	5	3	4	2	8	1
2	4	8	6	3	5	1	7
5	3	7	1	2	4	6	8
3	6	4	8	7	1	5	2
7	1	2	5	8	6	3	4

Puzzle 55: Coin Board

A)

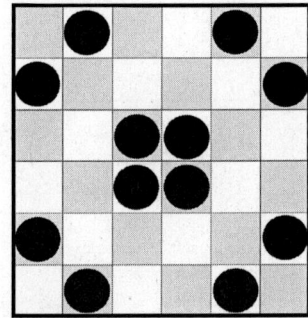

B)

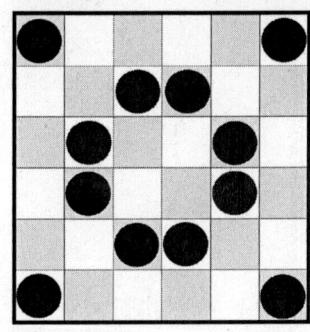

Bonus Game: Tic-Tac-Toe

O		X
		X
O	X	O

The next **O** is placed in the top left corner of the puzzle so that even if the other player places an **X** in the left middle square to block you, you can still place an **O** in the centre square and win (or vice versa).

Puzzle 56: Word Swirl
1. Pilot
2. Polar
3. Topic
4. Plot
5. Cop
6. Pair
7. Pit
8. Portal
9. Patio
10. Pact

Bonus: Tropical

Puzzle 57: Folding Cubes
B and C

Puzzle 58: Word Search– C

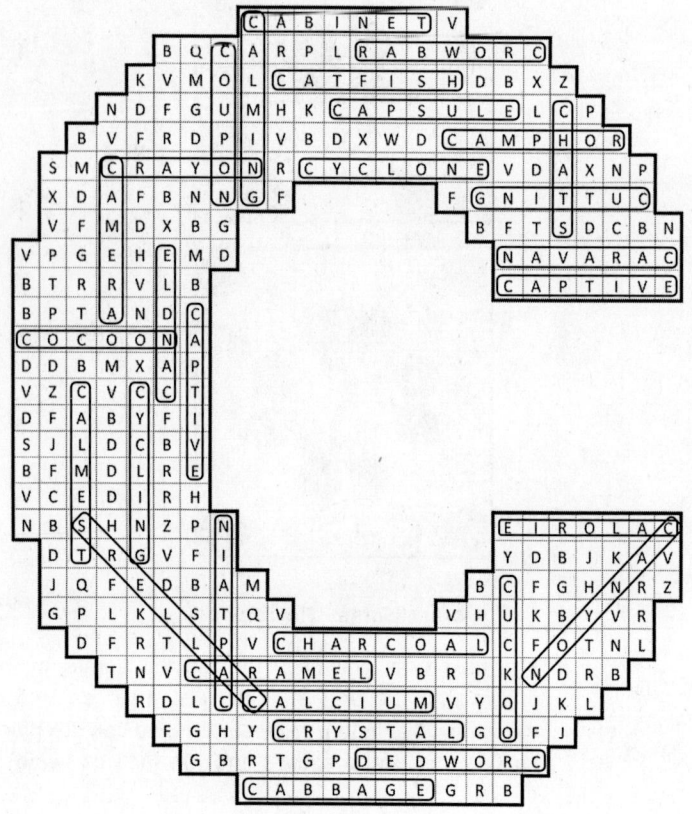

Bonus Puzzle

Jemima is the oldest friend and should get the extra slice of pizza. If Suzy is two months older than Jane, then Jemima is three months older than Jane and one month older than Suzy. Elizabeth is younger than both Suzy and Jemima. Therefore, Jemima is the oldest.

Puzzle 59: Slitherlinks

A)

B)

Bonus: Rebus Puzzle

1. Once upon a time.
2. Diamond ring.
3. Equally important.
4. White elephant.

Puzzle 60: Jobs and Careers Reverse Crossword

W	E	B	D	E	V	E	L	O	P	E	R	
			O									
	E		C		A							
	V	E	T	E	R	I	N	A	R	I	A	N	D
	E		O		C			C					E
	N		R		H			C	A	P	T	A	I	N
	T				I			O					T
	P	I	L	O	T			U			P		I
	L				E			N		P	A		S
	A		R	E	C	E	P	T	I	O	N	I	S	T
	N				T			A		L		N	
A	N	A	L	Y	S	T		N		I		T	
	E							T		C	L	E	R	K
A	R	T	I	S	T					E		R	

Puzzle 61: Word Pyramid

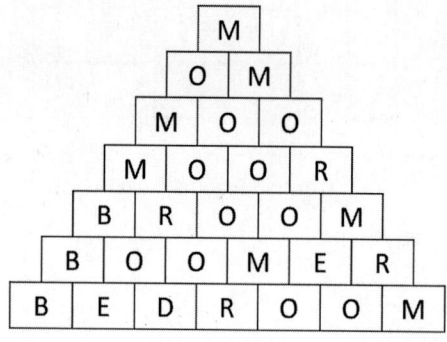

Bonus Game: Boredom and Broomed.

Puzzle 62: Loopy Loops (possible solution)

Bonus Game: Missing Vowels (possible solutions)

1. Future/After
2. Civil
3. School
4. Dated/Doted
5. Dream/Dorm/Dram/Drum

Puzzle 63: What Comes Next?
Option D is the correct answer. The single black square keeps moving from right to left and back to right in each cross while the black rectangle moves in a clockwise direction starting from the top, to the right, to the bottom and so on.

Bonus Game: Find the Odd One Out
1. Fish. The others can live on land as well as in water.
2. Piano. The others are stringed instruments.
3. Gloves. All the others are worn on feet.
4. 25. The other numbers are even numbers.
5. Cabbage. The others are fruits.

Puzzle 64: Word Squares

A)
S	H	O	T
H	A	V	E
O	V	E	N
T	E	N	T

B)
H	O	M	E
O	P	E	N
M	E	N	D
E	N	D	S

Puzzle 65: Word Circles
1. Accident
2. Division
3. Platform
4. Strength
5. Umbrella
6. Disclose
7. Hospital
8. Stunning
9. Wildlife
10. Tomorrow

Puzzle 66: Reverse Minesweeper

 💣	2		0		0		 💣	3
2	 💣						 💣	 💣
	2	 💣		0			2	2
0			2			2		0
		0		 💣	 💣	 💣		
		2	4	 💣	8	 💣	3	0
	 💣	 💣		 💣	 💣	 💣		1
 💣	3			3	4		2	 💣
 💣	2		0		 💣		1	

Bonus Game: Code Decode

1. Baby
2. Cool
3. Fact
4. Game
5. Quip/Join

Puzzle 67: Matching Shapes

Puzzle 68: Tangram

Bonus Game: Anagrams

1. Shrub   2. Seals   3. Dairy   4. Moor   5. Stew

Puzzle 69: Dividing Shapes

A)

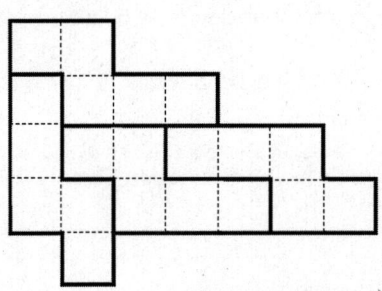

B)

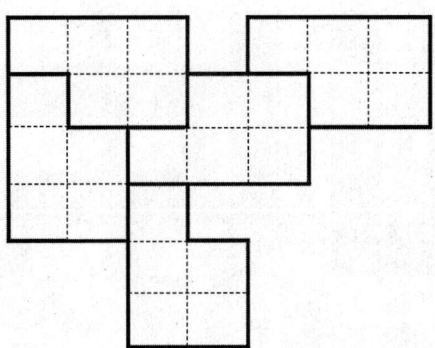

Bonus Game: Connect Loops

Puzzle 70: Code Decode
A) Cabin, Villa, Apartment, Hut
B) Gardening, Fishing, Crochet, Art
C) Accent, Pitch, Tone, Diction

Puzzle 71: Counting Cubes
A) 12 Cubes– 5 on the bottom row, 5 in the middle row and 2 at the top.
B) 19 Cubes– 9 on the bottom row, 5 in the middle row and 5 at the top.

Riddle Me This

The answer is Sun.

Puzzle 72: Crossword Groups

Puzzle 73: Hashi

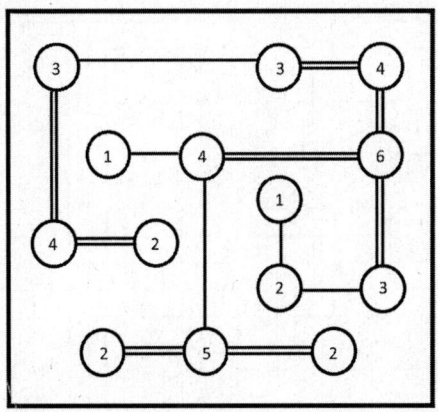

Puzzle 74: Letter Slides

A) Wart
B) Straw
C) Star
D) Water
E) Bear
F) Wear
G) Rate
H) Wet
I) Berry
J) Strawberry

Bonus Game: Number Slides

1	2	3	4
12	11	10	5
13	16	9	6
14	15	8	7

Puzzle 75: Math Whiz

A) 45
B) 10
C) 11

What Comes Next?

55 comes next. Add 10 to each number to get the next number.

Puzzle 76: Maze Amaze

Puzzle 77: Word Ladders

A)
H	E	A	D
H	E	A	L
T	E	A	L
T	E	L	L
T	A	L	L
T	A	I	L

B)
S	L	O	W
L	L	O	T
S	O	O	T
S	O	O	N
S	O	W	N
D	O	W	N

Bonus Game: Assembling a Word Square

P	L	O	T
L	A	V	A
O	V	A	L
T	A	L	E

Puzzle 78: Domino Twist

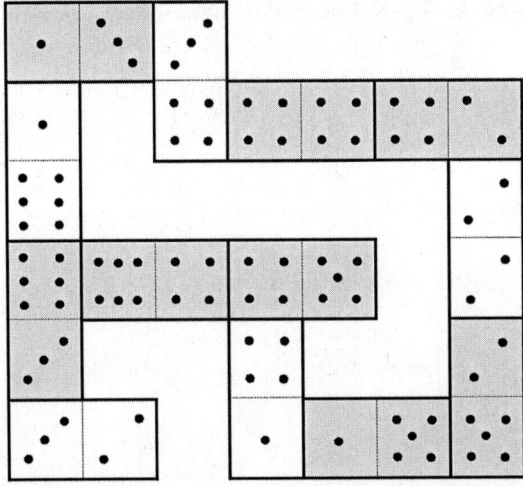

Puzzle 79: Sudoku

7	6	2	4	5	1	9	8	3
9	4	8	7	6	3	2	1	5
5	3	1	2	9	8	4	7	6
6	1	3	8	4	2	7	5	9
2	9	7	6	3	5	8	4	1
8	5	4	1	7	9	6	3	2
4	7	9	3	1	6	5	2	8
3	2	6	5	8	4	1	9	7
1	8	5	9	2	7	3	6	4

Bonus Game: Opposites Attract

H U M B L E

P R O U D

Puzzle 80: Coin Board

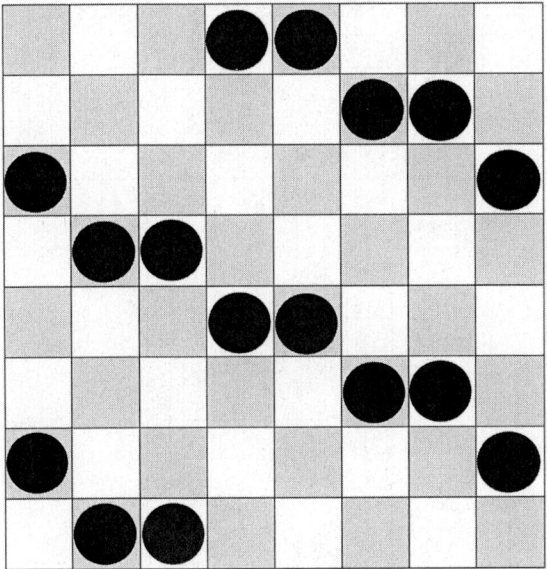

Whodunnit?

If Thomas was attacked from behind, he could not have noticed the attacker's V-neck sweater since the V-neck is at the front of the sweater.

Puzzle 81: Word Swirl
1. Sewing
2. Genie
3. Swing
4. Wings
5. Pigs
6. Wig
7. Sign
8. Swig
9. Weeping
10. Sweeping

Puzzle 82: Folding Cubes
A and D

Puzzle 83: Word Search– T

Puzzle 84: Slitherlinks

A)

		2	3	3	3	2	0	
0		2		1		2		
1		2		1		0	2	1
3	2		2	3	1			2
	2	3		1	0			3
2	0	1				0		3
2		0				1		3
2	1	1	0	1			1	
3		3	3	2	1		0	

B)

3	2	2	2		1		2	2
2		1		0			3	3
2			1			1	2	
2		2	1	2			1	2
2		1	0		1		1	2
3	2		1	2		1	2	
2		2				1	2	1
		2	3	3		0		2
2	2	1		1	2	1		2

Puzzle 85: Foodie Reverse Crossword

Bonus Game: Anagrams

1. Palm
2. Fried
3. Dusty
4. Melon
5. Grin

Puzzle 86: Word Pyramid

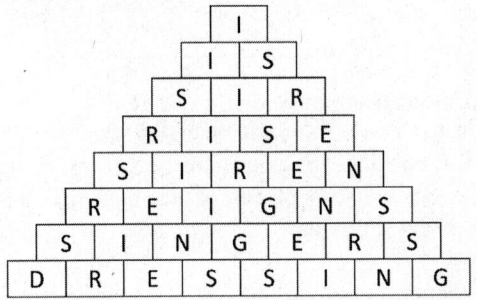

Bonus Puzzle: Code Decode

Each word is an anagram of four different cities– Oslo, Paris, Athens and Geneva.

Puzzle 87: Loopy Loops (possible solution)

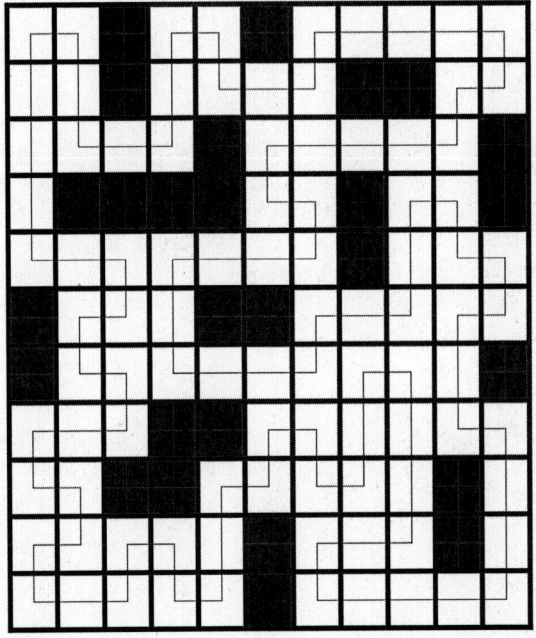

> **Riddle Me This**
>
> Glass!

Puzzle 88: What Comes Next?

Option B is the correct answer. In every row, the star moves two places to the right, the black square and black triangle move one place to the left and two places to the right and the grey square moves one place to the left.

Puzzle 89: Word Squares

A	D	U	L	T
D	I	N	A	R
U	N	I	T	E
L	A	T	T	E
T	R	E	E	S

> **Bonus Game: Word Finder (possible words)**
>
> Material, area, aria, earl, item, lair, lama, lame, late, lati, lear, liar, lima, lime, lira, lire, lite, mail, mare, male, malt, mara, mare, mart, mate, meal, meat, melt, meta, mile, mire, mite, rail, rale, rate, real, ream, rial, rile, rime, rite, tail, tale, tali, tame, tear, teal, team, tare, term, tier, tile, time, tire, tram, trim.

Puzzle 90: Word Circles

1. Abandoned
2. Backflips
3. Dangerous
4. Generated
5. Schoolbag
6. Abilities
7. Captivity
8. Dashboard
9. Rainwater
10. Telephone

Puzzle 91: Reverse Minesweeper

1	1						💣	2	💣
2	💣		0	0					
💣						💣		0	
💣	3	0		💣	4	💣	2		
💣			2	💣		2		0	
			2		2	💣		0	
0		💣	💣			2	3		
		2		1	1	💣	💣	3	
💣	2	0		0			4	💣	💣
💣						0		💣	3

Bonus: Rebus Puzzle

1. Bad intentions.
2. Too big to ignore. (2 big 2 ignore)
3. Comfortable (come 4 table)
4. Street corner/corner street.

Puzzle 92: Matching Shapes

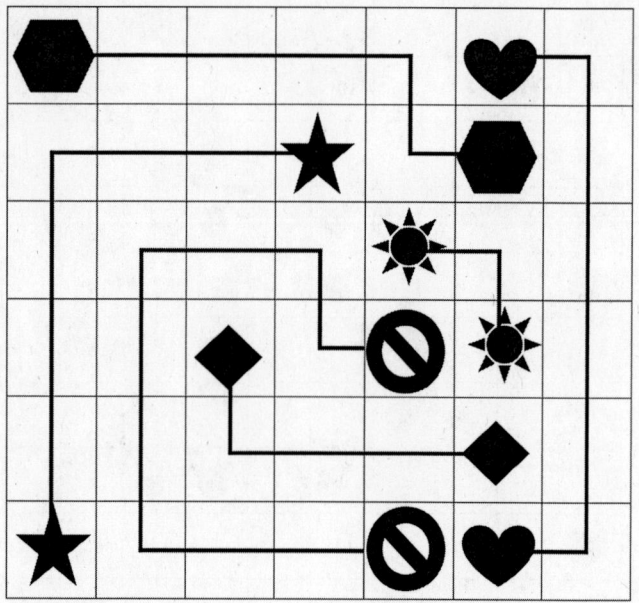

Puzzle 93: Tangram

> **Bonus Puzzle: Counting Squares**
>
> 10 squares– 1 large, 1 in the middle, 4 medium squares and 4 small squares.

Puzzle 94: Dividing Shapes

A)

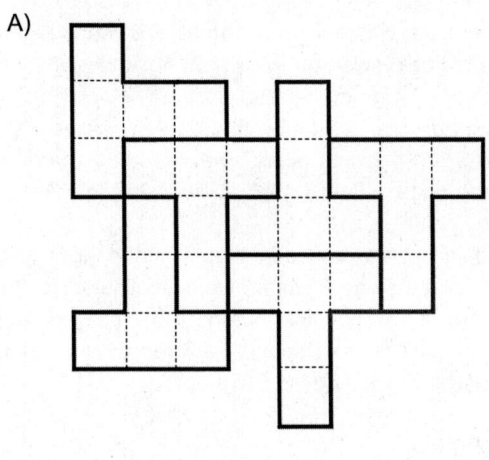

B)

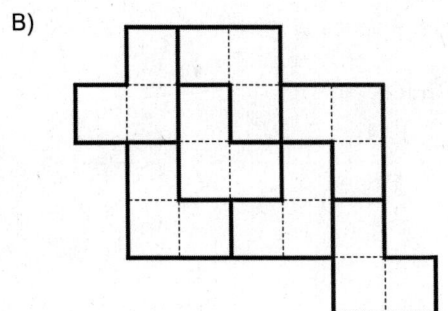

Puzzle 95: Code Decode
1. Mary had a little lamb
2. Couch potato
3. SOS
4. Time
5. Hopscotch

Bonus Puzzle: Code Decode

961 is the code to unlock the suitcase lock.
1. The first clue eliminates three numbers: 3,8 and 7.
2. If we eliminate the 7 and 8 from the second clue (because of Clue 1), we now know that 1 is the right digit in the right place. Therefore, the final code is ___ ___ 1.
3. Moving to the third clue, we know that 3 and 8 are wrong digits. Therefore, 6 is the right answer; but we still do not know whether it is the first or second digit in the final code.
4. Moving to the fourth clue, we know that 7 is a wrong digit. Therefore, 1 and 9 are the right digits. We also know that 1 is the last digit in the code. We still don't know if 9 is the first or second digit.
5. Going by the fifth clue, we can see that 9 is the right digit and in its correct place since 8 and 3 were eliminated in the first clue. Therefore, if 9 is the first number and 1 is the last number, then the middle number should be 6 (according to the third clue). Therefore, the answer is 961.

Puzzle 96: Counting Cubes
There are 27 cubes in total— 9 cubes in 3 rows.

Riddle Me This

A mirror!

Puzzle 97: Crossword School

Puzzle 98: Hashi

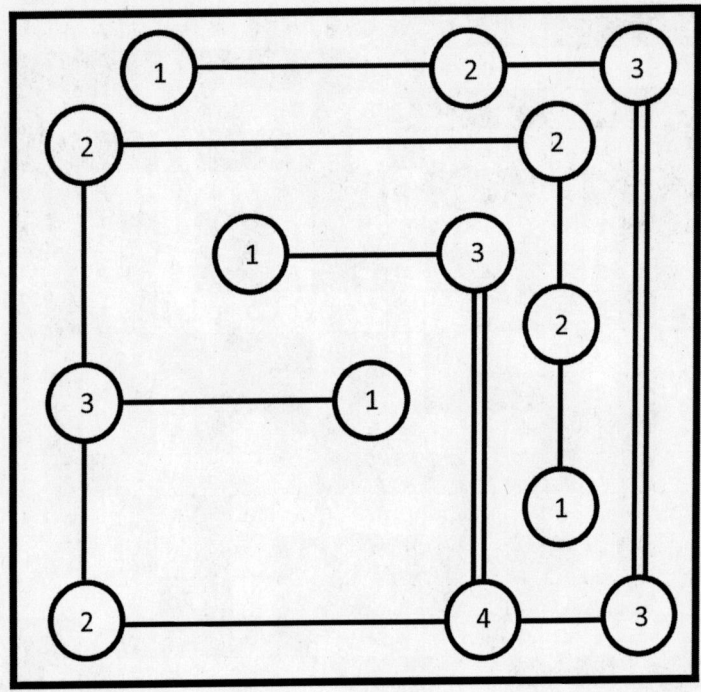

Puzzle 99: Letter Slides
A) Red
B) Fire
C) Spine
D) Pine
E) Hind
F) Dips
G) Hip
H) Fried
I) Hide
J) Friendship

Bonus Puzzle: First and Last

A	P	P	R	O	A	C	H
C	H	A	I	R	M	A	N
A	N	N	O	U	N	C	E
C	E	L	L	U	L	A	R
A	R	T	I	S	T	I	C

Puzzle 100: Math Whiz
A) 2
B) 10
C) 15

What Comes Next?

34 is the answer. Add the previous number to get the next number. Therefore,
1 + 2 = 3
3 + 2 = 5
5 + 3 = 8
8 + 5 = 13
13 + 8 = 21
21 + 13 = 34.

ACKNOWLEDGEMENTS

I would like to thank Yamini Chowdhury from Rupa Publications for this wonderful opportunity to write yet another book. Thank you to Vicky Sharma from Rupa Publications for meticulously editing this book. Special thanks goes to my husband Rabin Stephen, my daughters Shifrah and Annika and my parents Reginald Solomon and Shantha Solomon for their enduring love and support throughout the entire writing process.

Lots of love and gratitude goes to my younger daughter Annika Stephen for using her artistic skills to help me with some of the beautiful images in this book. I would also like to extend a big thank you to Geetanjali Kapoor and Derrick Thomas for helping me with some of the images and providing me with valuable technical know-how. I am very grateful to Rabin, Shifrah, Annika, Shantha Solomon, Regi Solomon, Suryakumari Dennison, Pradeep, Monali, Derrick, Ritabrata and all my other friends and family who took an active interest in this book and helped solve all the puzzles while painstakingly checking each puzzle for ambiguity and mistakes.

Thank you all!